STANDING
AND UNDERSTANDING

STANLEY BRICE FROST

———

Standing
and Understanding

A RE-APPRAISAL OF THE
CHRISTIAN FAITH

———

MONTREAL
McGILL UNIVERSITY PRESS

Library of Congress No. 68-59095

PRINTED IN GREAT BRITAIN
BY THE WHITEFRIARS PRESS LIMITED
LONDON AND TONBRIDGE

FOR

DAVID AND PAULINE
AND VALERIE

A NEW GENERATION

As Yahweh the God of Israel lives, before
    whom I stand. . . .

ELIJAH

And having done all to stand, stand then
    with your loins girded with truth. . . .

ST PAUL

Here I stand. I can do no other. So help
    me God.

LUTHER

I will light in your heart a lamp of
    understanding.

2 ESDRAS

I am building in the human understanding
    a true model of the world.

BACON

CONTENTS

PREFACE

I AM GRATEFUL to the Trustees of the Arthur Samuel Peake Memorial Trust for their invitation to give the 1968 Lecture, and particularly that the invitation was conveyed to me by my friend of student days at Richmond and in Marburg, Dr Percy Scott.

The first volume of biblical scholarship to come into my possession was given me by my brother on my seventeenth birthday. It was Peake's *Critical Introduction to the New Testament*. I read it with astonishment, for I had been brought up in a conservative piety, but also with delight, for here was an honesty and an intelligence the like of which I had not previously met in religious studies. I never to my great regret had the privilege of meeting Peake (he died the year before I received his *Introduction*) but through that book he greatly influenced me to find in biblical studies an intellectual challenge and an abiding fascination. It is indeed an honour and a privilege to be invited to take part in the annual remembrance of this good and fine scholar.

I at first intended to offer a strictly biblical subject, but I soon discovered that there was already conceived within me another book, which would not be denied gestation and birth. Remembering Peake's own *Christianity, its Nature and its*

9

Truth, I persuaded myself and the Trustees that what I now had in mind would be a not inappropriate contribution, and I have laboured to produce it. Yet now I offer it with very real misgivings for I have been led into many fields that are not my own.

The circumstances are these. By unexpected ways I have been brought to a position in which I am concerned with the administration of a very large, very active university. As a result I spend—to my regret—little time with colleagues in Divinity, but I spend long hours—to my great enrichment—with all the many varieties of academics who contribute to the rich confusion of a modern university campus.

This experience, now extended over six years, has inevitably left its mark on me. I see theology and religion, not only from within, as a believer, but also from without, as a modern sceptic, to whom nothing is indubitable and only truth is sacred. The question has forced itself upon me: Is it possible to accept the modern account of the human situation and remain intelligently and with integrity a christian?

This book was written in part as an attempt to find an answer to that question and to discover what point I myself had reached. Any reader who might happen to recall my neo-orthodox days (my first printed piece was entitled 'Dogmatize or Perish', an answer to the then current catchword, 'Evangelize or Perish') will recognize that I have travelled far. Some will say that I have travelled too far—that I am no longer truly a christian. Others will slap me on the label 'Liberal Protestant *Redivivus*', and thereby dismiss me out of hand. But I believe the issues are too fundamental to be settled by mere name-calling. My more important purpose is to plead that christian theologians must be aware of the world around them, and that being in the fashion theologically is no substitute for ensuring that beliefs are consonant with the modern account of man and his universe. This is not simply the question

of 'religion and science'. It is the larger matter of ensuring that
theological thought is of one piece with all the rest of man's
thinking. Theology has lived too long (as Harnack prophesied
it would, if Barth's theology should prevail)[1] in a world of its
own, and that world is becoming more and more a world of
unreality. We cannot by dogma make the round world flat,
and theology cannot patronise the idea of evolution and think
that it will thereby be tamed. If philosophers of history have
dissolved the concept of history from which the idea of a
revelation in history derives, no theological subtlety can
circumvent that fact. Theology cannot be intellectually
isolationist. I have been attempting over the past several years
to say these things in a number of papers,[2] and I now welcome
the opportunity to put my ideas together in one presentation.
It is probable that my own attempt to explore the relationship
of christian teaching to the basic ideas of our time will be
judged by the best critics to be very inadequate, but if it
encourages someone else, or even better, a number of other
people, who have more leisure and more natural advantages
than I, to perform the task more competently, my effort will
not have been unsuccessful.

I have called this book *Standing and Understanding* because
this title reflects the foci of my discussion—the standpoint
from which I have to begin, and the attempt to apprehend the
data with which I am confronted. The verb 'to understand'
clearly conceals a metaphor or mental picture, the detail and

[1] See note 2 to chapter I.

[2] Cf. especially 'The Theologian and Contemporary Thought', the
Presidential Address to the American Association of Theological Schools,
1964, *Theological Education*, I, 1, 1964, pp. 3–14; 'Reviewing Some Founda-
tions', in *Horizons of Theological Education*, a volume presented to Charles
Taylor, ed. J. Ziegler, Dayton, 1966, pp. 23–34; and 'Church and University',
in *The Church in the Modern World*, a volume presented to James Sutherland
Thomson, ed. G. Johnston and W. Roth, Toronto, 1967, pp. 185–202. I
have used some of the ideas presented in these papers in sections of the
present book.

origin of which has been lost.[3] To 'stand under' or 'before'
(the German equivalent is not *unterstehen* but *verstehen*) a
situation was probably intended to convey the idea of standing
back from it and surveying it in order to relate it to one's
previously acquired body of knowledge, and in order to orient
one's self towards it. The result looked for is reflected in the
colloquial phrase 'we now know where we stand about it'.
This it seems to me is aptly descriptive of the human situation:
we need to know where we stand, and we need to know 'where
we stand about', well, about everything: we stand and we
need to understand.

I make no apology for the fact that the longest chapter,
indeed the latter half of the book, is concerned with Jesus.
Christianity which is not centred in him is indeed *Hamlet*
lacking the Prince of Denmark. It is inevitable that any personal
re-appraisal of the christian faith should be intensely interested
in Jesus—particularly as regards the dependability of the
sources of our knowledge of him, and as regards the estimate
which we make of him as a person. These will always be central
questions for the christian and for the Church, and I have
tried to come to terms with them.

I could not attempt this kind of a book without a very great
deal of help. The number of names in the Index which are
those of colleagues, past and present, of former students and
of friends in two continents, reveals something of my indebted-
ness. I am particularly grateful to the members of the Faculty
of Graduate Studies and Research of McGill University for

[3] *The Oxford English Dictionary* gives the Old English *understondan* and
Old Frisian *understonda*, so the metaphor is very old. In German *sich unterstehen* means 'to undertake, venture, dare', and the meaning of 'comprehend'
has been taken over by *verstehen*, 'to stand before'. But in English the force
of the preposition 'under' was at one time as much 'before', 'beside', as it
was 'beneath'; cf. the place-name 'Newcastle-under-Lyme', the Lyme being
a small river. Similarly Dutch *verstaan* and Scandinavian *forstå* also point
back to the very distant metaphor of standing in front of something in order
to bring it into mental focus.

their colleagueship over the past nine years but especially during the past six in which I have served as Dean of the Faculty. They have taught me more than I shall ever be conscious of having learnt. Particular thanks are due to Professors Charles Adams, Director of the Islamic Institute, David Bates, Chairman of the Department of Physiology, Maxwell Dunbar, Director of the Marine Sciences Centre and my Associate Dean, and G. A. Woonton, Chairman of the Department of Physics, for having read a first draft of the manuscript, and for having given me very helpful comments. The errors that remain are all my own. I also have to thank very sincerely Mrs Anice Baird, my secretary, who amidst many other pressures, has typed and re-typed with unfailing readiness.

Montreal
Christmas 1967   STANLEY BRICE FROST

Chapter One

THE PLACE OF STANDING

MAN stands on a shrinking planet in an expanding universe.

We know little of his history. He is a relative newcomer to the world scene. He emerged from the swamps of the Tigris–Euphrates valley six or seven thousand years ago, though of course there are traces of his scattered primitive settlements reaching back another two or three thousand years. His original habitat is obscure, but it may have been Africa, a hundred thousand or even, according to J. B. Leaky's latest speculations, twenty million years ago. Clearly, he spread widely as a species, and we have early traces of him in places as far apart as Europe and China. But he began to show signs of having outstanding abilities only a few thousand years ago, when he began to organise himself into the proto-civilisations of first Mesopotamia, then Egypt and the Punjab. Since then his advance towards world-domination has been swift, ruthless and unchallenged.

We have a barely adequate but at least continuous record of his intellectual life from roughly five thousand years ago. From this we can trace the steady expansion of his horizons, from the flat plains of the Land of the Two Rivers, to the Fertile Crescent including Upper and Lower Egypt, to the coastlands of the Mediterranean, to Britain and India, to

14

Europe, Asia and America; and finally the globe. At every stage, as it grew progressively bigger, it was his world, and his latest metropolis was the centre of it.

Recently, however, his perspectives have undergone a violent change. Not Babylon, nor Rome, nor London, not even Los Angeles, is the centre of his world. It has no centre. The earth itself is no centre, but revolves around the sun. Even the sun, he has learned, is not central, but lies apparently in the outer reaches of one of the rings of a vast spiral of similar suns and planets, while other equally huge systems are disappearing in all directions at unimaginable speeds. Man has discovered with something like horror that he is living in an exploding universe.

Simultaneously, his planet is shrinking. The mass communication media and the tightening strings of the world's airlines are contracting the globe into one megapolis, if not into one village. The culture of the western world is spreading everywhere and the same music, the same idols, the same affluent-society values, are rampant in Moscow, Lagos, Tokyo and New York. The distant East is no longer distant, and a Hindu temple may be in Benares or it may be in a Caribbean island, but it may equally well be in a back-street in Birmingham. The man who rides the commuter in a western city may be an active episcopalian or he may be a devout muslim or a vague buddhist. The world is shrinking and all men and all faiths are being thrown, whether they like it or not, closely into each other's company.

This double change of perspective, a shrinking planet and an expanding universe, is having a profound effect upon the thought-processes of the species. While there is as yet considerable diversity still remaining, nevertheless the mental attitude which is spreading swiftly may be described as a disillusionment with all authorities. Hitherto men have accepted certain beliefs unquestioningly. They were in the Bible or in the Qur'an or they were the teaching of Confucius or of the Buddha and they were to be believed. Now, however, sacred scriptures are seen as the anthology of the ideas and beliefs of men of earlier generations, interesting but not likely to be any more true with regard to their spiritual apprehensions than they are with regard to their cosmological speculations. The great teachers of the past were men of fine insight but limited inevitably by the narrow horizons of their times. With his authorities devalued, man finds that everything is for speculation and nothing is for sure.

As we look back on man's long climb, whether it be over ten thousand years or twenty million, we realise that only quite recently, within the last century, has he come to anything like a true awareness of his position. Even now it is still true that he knows a very great deal about his world and the universe, and remarkably little about himself. Even his physical evolution is shrouded in mystery. There is something absurd, something disturbing, something vaguely sinister about his inability to discover very much about himself. We are tempted to borrow a paragraph or two from the novels of Mr Graham Greene and see *homo sapiens* as a hunted creature. He has been stumbling for untold years along dark passages, taking many a bruise and tumble, but always picking himself up and pushing desperately on. He has turned many wrong corners but has always felt his way painfully back to the turn; he has been lost in vast caverns where he circled round and round, seemingly endlessly in the dark, until the happy day he fell through a hole and found himself on the march once more. He was always pushing on, never able to stop for more than a short while, driven forward by some nameless horror behind, lured on by some equally nameless hope ahead. But now he has emerged into a large cave and away out there, beyond its mouth, he can see daylight. But he dare not go forward. Before he does, he must find out. He must know who he is, and how he came to be stumbling in those galleries deep in the mountain, and why it was so important to keep going when every muscle clamoured for rest. What is it he is expecting out there? Will he still be alone, or is there someone, out there, waiting for him? If so, is it a friend, or is it an enemy? He does not know. All he is sure of is that he daren't go forward until he does know. He must try to remember. Where did he come from? How did he come to be in the mountain? Above all, who is he?

As he stands there, shrinking back against the wall of the cave, hopeful and fearful in turn, he begins to hear voices, many voices. They are all giving him advice, contradictory advice. Go forward, go back, stand still, run. Some whisper seductively, others are strident in their self-commendation, and others again are hectoring, seeking to command. Which are self-deluded fools, pretending a wisdom they do not have, and which are malicious liars, seeking to destroy him, and which if any may be telling the truth, he does not know. One thing he does know, and that is that it has been only his own determination, his own courage and his own intelligence, which have got him as far as this. The only person he can trust is himself.

This, then, is the human situation as, I venture to suggest, the great majority of intelligent men and women now see it. In today's world we may fairly term it not the human situation but the human predicament. To those of us brought up securely in the christian tradition it is as fantastically unreal as the nightmare experiences of an amnesiac agent in a tale of espionage. But if we are to re-appraise our faith and test it thoroughly, we must do so in what modern man believes to be the realities of the situation. It has to be re-appraised in a ruthless world, where nothing is taken for granted, nothing is assumed, nothing is given, where everything has to be examined, and everything has to be established and the only risks to be taken are the calculated ones.

Against that background, I want to make in this chapter

four major points. First, that for our generation there can be no other beginning for thought than man himself. 'Man is the question he asks about himself'.[1] We cannot be, any of us, other than humanist in our thinking. This has been, I know, theologically unfashionable for a long time, but the unhappy thing about christian theology, especially in its prevalent protestant forms, has been its alienation from the generality of human thinking. While lawyers and artists and biologists and physicists have been together building a new world-view, which they could to a large extent share and talk about together, the theologian has been off in a little world all his own. He has asserted certain unquestionable 'truths', such as 'revelation', 'the christ-event', 'the word of God'. But the moderns, the philosopher and the scientist and the historian and the rest, are not impressed with oracular assertions, not even those of a Karl Barth,[2] and indeed are generally quite ignorant of the

---

[1] Paul Tillich, *Systematic Theology*, Chicago 1951, Vol. 1, p. 62. That mine is, even theologically-speaking, a not wholly reprehensible approach to the human situation is indicated by the following from John Macquarrie: 'Whether we are Christians or secularists, we share our humanity. Is this then the common ground from which a theological interpretation can begin today? Christianity is a doctrine of man as well as of God. John Calvin, as is well known, having remarked that true and solid wisdom consists almost entirely of two parts, the knowledge of God and the knowledge of ourselves, went on to say that "as these are connected together with many ties, it is not easy to determine which of the two precedes and gives birth to the other". Calvin himself began with the doctrine of God, and this is probably the logical place to begin, and was also an intelligible beginning in an age when most people took religion very seriously and could discourse in a theological idiom. But in a secular age, we have to consider the alternative.' *Studies in Christian Existentialism*, Montreal, 1965, p. 4. John Macquarrie is Professor of Systematic Theology, Union Theological Seminary, New York.

[2] Harnack's fear that if Barth's theological standpoint came to be widely shared, theology would be driven from the university as a subject of serious discussion has very largely come true. (cf. 'An Open Letter to Karl Barth', *Christliche Welt*, March 8, 1923). I owe this reference to Dr H. Martin Rumscheidt, a former student of mine, whose doctoral thesis was entitled: *Revelation and Theology—An Analysis of the Barth-Harnack Correspondence of 1923* (National Library, Ottawa, 1967). Cf. pp. 35, 49. Barth's distinction between 'religion' (which he denigrates) and 'revelation' (which he applauds) (Dogmatic I, 1, 2, § 17) is a mere playing with labels. What distinguishes 'the

prevailing fashions of theology. They do know that while neo-orthodox protestants talk one way, catholics talk another, and that very intelligent and sincere muslims talk another, and that hindus, whose capacity for abstract intellectualism has never been in doubt, talk in quite a different way. Religion can proffer no claim to self-authenticating revelation which by reason of a unanimous testimony compels acceptance of its testimony. On the contrary, religion offers a bewildering variety of concepts, a series of contradictions and inconsistencies which have led many sincere men to dismiss it from serious consideration altogether. Others recognise that the quantity, if not the quality, of the evidence is impressive, and are prepared to reserve judgement until a reasonable assessment can be made. But by that very reasonableness, they emphasise their humanist position. Man is indeed the judge of all things and he has to take all the evidence he can find, weigh it carefully, consider it closely, and then make his reasonable choice.

This means that man has only one at all dependable guide, and that is his power to reason. This is my second point and again it is not a very fashionable thought. Artists are almost unanimously loud in their condemnation. In the realm of the plastic arts, of the visual arts, even of music, and certainly of the novel and drama, we appear to be witnessing a headlong flight from reason. We are also told by psychiatrists that 'the games we play' are irrational, and that they deceive us more than they deceive others, and are motivated by emotional drives of which the conscious mind takes good care to be unaware. We act, they insist, by unreason rather than reason. Wilfred

---

Gospel' from 'religion'? Who other than Barth can tell us what is 'revelation' and what is merely man-made 'religion'? Barth is in fact more of a humanist than most, because he arrogates to himself the rôle of arbiter in no uncertain manner. Cf. Paul Tillich, *Christianity and The Encounter of World Religions*, New York and London, 1963, pp. 44–46, and C. J. Bleeker, *Christ in Modern Athens*, Leiden, 1965, pp. 90–98. Dr Bleeker is Professor of the History and Phenomenology of Religions in the University of Amsterdam.

Cantwell Smith recently made a perceptive comment on this point: 'In the past, all atheism in the West has in effect been in the name of Greece, against Palestine. It is the rationalist, the philosopher, who has argued that religion is false: reason versus faith . . . . More accurately, one should see it as a debate not between reason and faith, but between a faith in reason and a faith in God; or, more historically, between faith through the Greek heritage of Western civilisation, and faith through the Judaeo-Christian heritage. The standard Western position has comprised the two faiths together, whether in tension or in balance; but occasionally persons have arisen to argue that they are incompatible, so that men must have only one. Now the great dénouement of the twentieth century has been that faith in each of the traditions has petered out. Many artists and novelists and thinkers have lost not only faith in God, but faith in reason. They see behind the flux of phenomena neither an ultimate Person, creator, redeemer, judge, nor a rational order, a meaningful cosmic structure in relation to which, and in terms of which, meaning for human life can be formulated. Metaphysics is in even more total collapse today than is theology. Modern philosophy departments in general, and linguistic analysis in particular, are what is left of the philosophic tradition, once those practising it have lost their faith in a transcendent truth'.[3] But it needs to be remembered that this flight from reason is not characteristic of the natural and physical sciences; in them we rely as much as ever on logic and argument and hypothesis, and on the rationality of the universe; and we do so with remarkable success. The sciences provide us with an experimental demonstration of the dependability of reason. It is arguable, therefore, that the flight from reason in the arts, in the humanities, in philosophy and in

[3] *Questions of Religious Truth*, New York, 1967, pp. 25–26. Professor Smith, formerly my colleague at McGill, is now Director of the Center for the Study of World Religions at Harvard.

theology, is due simply to a temporary failure of nerve, and that in the total human situation we must have the courage to re-assert our faith in reason.[4]

In any case, however unfashionable and however fallible reason may be, we have to follow its lead, simply because it is the only guide we have. True, we have to be constantly on our guard with it. We cannot, for example, define reason; we can only watch it suspiciously and follow its guidance cautiously. That in terms of abstract numerals, two and two make four is indeed something we accept without cavil; if somebody then says that two raindrops and two raindrops do not make four but one, we are not disturbed because reason can cope with the recognition that if the statement is to remain true the twos and the four have to retain, not merge, their identities. That if A equals B and B equals C, then C must equal A is again, we recognise, good reasoning; but we further recognise that if the letters stand for persons, then the equality will not be absolute but will refer only to some particular aspect of these persons— that they all hold the same rank in the Navy, for example. But in other situations, in home life, shall we say, the three persons will be very unalike. Reason itself recognises its own limitations, and does not always blindly follow strict logic. It is aware of the need to allow for emotional factors and will often give weight to so-called 'instinctive judgements'—though these are generally explicable as pattern-reactions based on a similarity of situation, and are due to accumulated experience, and thus may very reasonably be given considerable weight; but when all provisos have been allowed for, it is with reason that we are left, to follow as our guide. We have to; we have no other.

[4] In saying this I reveal my spiritual inheritance from John Wesley, who on one side of his nature was very much the disciple of John Locke. Cf. his *Earnest Appeal to Men of Reason and Religion* and his *Farther Appeal* (*Works*, London, 1830, Volume VIII, pp. 1–247). I discovered this Wesley characteristic (to my considerable surprise) thirty years ago when I wrote my doctoral thesis *Die Autoritätslehre in den Werken John Wesleys*, Munich 1938.

It is this understanding of the human situation which has given the prevailing philosophy of our times the description 'existentialist'. Like most neat little labels it covers a multitude of variants, while nevertheless indicating a common characteristic which is the dominating and significant one. In this case the label indicates the common recognition that man is no detached observer of life, but is himself involved in it, facing daily with his own resources practical situations and, indeed, ultimate issues, with regard to which he has to make decisions. In making these decisions, man can only try to be as reasonable as the circumstances will permit. Plato's picture of man's nature, in which the chariot of his being was drawn by the two strong horses of 'appetite' and 'spirit' but whereof the charioteer was 'reason', was not, as a metaphor, so very far off the mark, so long as we recognise that 'reason' is not simply the logical faculty in man, but a broader, more sensitive apprehension which perhaps we might describe as man's critical faculties. At any rate, however we broaden or refine our description, man is guided by this reason. It is what has brought him so far along the road, and it is the only guide he dare follow for the future. If he is going to make anything of the human situation, it will be by argument and discussion, not by accepting authorities and pronouncements.

Nevertheless, let us not be in any doubt that the last word in religion as in all else is 'faith'. When all the considerations have been marshalled and assessed, one has to arrive at a judgement and then live by the assumption that that judgement is correct. As the argument of this book proceeds, I arrive at a number of places where I have to choose between one or other accounts of the situation; according to how I make that choice I am then faced with a further set of implications. In other words, I choose to believe certain propositions, and then exercise the faith that these propositions require of me. I choose (as reasonably as possible) to believe, and then I live in faith.

Faith and reason are not only compatible but are inseparable.

The third observation I want to make is the need to avail ourselves of all the knowledge which is available to us. To those who have not grown up with protestant theology over the last thirty or forty years it is incredible that there has been since the nineteen twenties a deep distrust, indeed, an outright refusal, of 'natural theology'.[5] During this same period, the increase of man's knowledge has been phenomenal. It has been calculated that it took from the time of Christ to 1750 to double the total knowledge of mankind, but that by 1900 it had doubled again; that it had doubled yet again by 1950, and that in the fifteen years from 1950–1965 it had redoubled once more. What yardstick is employed in such comparisons, I do not know, but at least they bring home vividly to us the fantastic proportions and speed of the 'knowledge explosion'—and there is every reason to think that the process will accelerate. Man is learning more and more about his universe, and more and more about himself. It is incredible that this vast increase of awareness has nothing to say about the ultimate issues of his existence. On the contrary, it is because of the new perspectives now opened up to us, and the vastly deepened insights now available to us, that I at least am faced with the need to re-appraise the christian position. Whatever the physical sciences, the biological sciences, the social and behavioural sciences, and the rich resources of the humanities, have to tell us about our own nature, our universe and our situation in that universe, will all have to be taken comprehensively into account. We cannot afford to neglect any source of knowledge.

[5] 'Natural Theology' may be a theology about nature, or a theology derived from nature. In neo-orthodox protestant thought, the former has been neglected but the latter has been shunned. The only good theology is 'revealed theology', that is, theology derived from the biblical revelation. The orthodox catholic position has been that man can derive so much by his reason from a consideration of nature, but that revelation then comes in to confirm and carry forward what reason has established. This has by and large been the position of the liberal protestant also.

It will be rejoined by many that even if such a programme were desirable it would be quite impossible. Knowledge is proliferating too fast. One biochemist has considerable difficulty in merely following the description of the research of another; what used to be blandly termed 'chemistry' is now dividing into a number of separate disciplines, of which the devotees are becoming so specialised, that a university department of 'chemistry' is hardly any longer possible; and the high-energy physicist and the solid-state physicist and the geo-physicist find it difficult even to talk a common language. This is not only true in the physical sciences, but is equally true in the biological sciences, while the social sciences are pretty well *terra incognita* to everyone outside their various fields of interest. Add to this the new and creative developments in law, the striking new insights in historiography, the re-evaluation of the creative imagination in the artistry of man, and the task becomes so immense that only a computer could begin to cope with it. Knowledge is getting beyond man's ability to reduce it to a meaningful whole.

It would be foolish to deny that this is a very weighty argument. No one man can properly assess the totality of the evidence before us at this time. But the notion that the new *deus ex machina* which can come to our rescue in this situation is the computer is a sadly mis-placed hope. The weighting of the various items that would have to be fed into the programme would require the kind of judgement which would pre-suppose the very answer we are looking for; we should in fact get out of the computer just what we had put in.[6] A computer is to the brain what a power-tool is to the hand, a microphone to the voice, or a television camera to the eye. But the wisdom or foolishness of the use we make of these extensions of our

---

[6] It is perhaps worthy of comment that my colleagues in the Computing Centre tell me that their most important code-word is GIGO—'garbage in, garbage out'. It is a salutary reminder.

natural facilities depends upon the judgement of the whole man. What any one individual has to do, then, is to recognise that he cannot be expert in all things, but that he can take an interest in the latest ideas to come out of, for example, particle physics, or out of the breaking of the genetic code, or in the attempts to distinguish patterns in social behaviour and to establish if not sociological laws then at least general rules; or again in the long-continued attempts to explain the behaviour of the individual in terms of a strict process of cause and effect. He can at least try to see why the practitioners of the visual arts have so fiercely rejected tradition, and ponder on the significance of this, and he can recognise the need to relate the present views of historiography to the claims made by the judaeo-christian tradition to a revelation 'in history'. So far from the theologian shutting himself up in the never-never land of Karl Barth's 'wonderful new world of the bible', he must of all men spend all his day on the university campus, wandering from lecture-hall to laboratory and from seminar to common-room, listening and learning, pondering and considering. At the end of the day, he must go home and put it all together into as meaningful a whole as he can, not least because if he will not do it, there is no one left in modern society to do it for him. The philosopher has abdicated the task, and is more intent on 'the philosphy of science', or 'the philosophy of history' and many another specialised inter-disciplinary study, or he is absorbed in the significance of language and how one makes any statement meaningfully. The day of the grand metaphysical system died with Hegel. Yet man's universe has to remain one, conceptually one, or he will himself become a schizophrenic. To the theologian, or perhaps one should say to the religious-minded man, must fall the task of being the generalist of our times. He may perform his rôle badly, but at least he does know that it has to be done.[7]

[7] It is significant that the one man of our time passionately interested in unifying the total experience of mankind was Teilhard de Chardin, a

The fourth point I want to make is that I am not hoping in this book to appraise all things, judge all things and arrive satisfyingly at ultimate and transcendent Reality. My aim is amibitious enough, but at least I am not foolish enough to think that I can penetrate all mysteries and arrive at absolute truth. Rather, I recognise that I am the product of the western, liberal-protestant, christian tradition, and that I cannot stand outside that tradition even if I so wanted. I can be an obscurantist christian or a disillusioned christian, or a lapsed christian, or an intelligent christian—or even a christian convert to another way of life—but I can never be other than a christian. I want if I can to be an intelligent christian: my friends are christian, my memories and my loves are christian, my hopes are christian. What I have to do, then, is to ask whether the tradition in which I have been brought up is still intellectually tenable, whether, in fact, it still offers a *modus vivendi* in our modern world. In another generation, the search for ultimate truth may be resumed. For this generation we have I think to recognise that Christianity is a myth, an interpretation of reality, and to ask whether as a myth it is still acceptable.

I use the controversial term 'myth' in this context very much in the way an economist or a physicist uses the term 'model'.

theologian who had received a scientific training and who was personally deeply religious. Cf. Paul Grenet, *Teilhard de Chardin, the Man and his Theories*, London and Toronto, 1965 (Fr. orig. Paris, 1961) and de Chardin's own work, particularly *The Phenomenon of Man*, London, 1959, (Fr. orig. *Le Phénomène Humain*, Paris, 1955). His religious apprehension was of a mystical nature and it seems to me that he tends to mythologise his scientific insights, but with his main endeavour I find myself deeply in sympathy. Cf. a letter written from China in 1934: "I am convinced that if Christianity has often had so much trouble in keeping its true place in the minds of believers, and also in winning the souls of the Gentiles, it is mainly because it sometimes gives the impression of scorning or fearing the grandeur and unity of our universe" (Grenet, *op. cit.* p. 139). Sir Julian Huxley thinks very highly of de Chardin and says of him (in the Introduction to *The Phenomenon of Man*), 'He has both clarified and unified our vision of reality'. But de Chardin does not commend himself to all his fellow scientists; cf. P. B. Medawar: *The Art of the Soluble*, 1967, p. 71f., for a highly critical review of *The Phenomenon of Man*.

An economist collects his data and assembles it into a coherent pattern, a construct of inter-acting forces, which he can set out descriptively in language or visually in graphs and diagrams, or mathematically in formulae. If the 'model' does not cope adequately with the realities of the on-going situation, he has toadapt and modify it until it performs more satisfactorily. Similarly a physicist has his data relating to molecules, atoms, and particles. He can visualise or depict them in 'models', or he can state their activity in mathematical formulae. When he is dealing with radiation he knowingly uses two unrelated if not mutually inconsistent models, that of energy as transmitted particles and that of energy as wave motion through space. Similarly I think we have to recognise that Christianity is of the nature of a 'model' of ultimate truth, and that it is, for this generation at least, a 'myth', that is, an interpretation of reality. Our task is to explore that myth, and discover whether it is sufficiently universal to absorb man's new knowledge and new insights and still satisfyingly interpret to him himself. We have to ask whether this myth can still cogently explain for him his past and still challengingly point him to his future. There is, as far as I can see, no present rival to Christianity, nor any successor of Christianity, as yet on the intellectual horizon. Therefore I have to stand in the christian tradition, but be ready to deepen and broaden and extend it to meet the demands of a new age. If I were a buddhist I would say the same, I think, of Buddhism, or if I were a muslim, the same of Islam. In this generation, each man must stand in his own tradition. For a human without a myth, lacking any interpretation of himself and his situation, may be a hominid or a humanoid, but he is less than a man: that is our modern way of expressing Plato's insight that the unexamined life is unlivable. Standing then in the christian tradition, I seek to discover, not the ontological truth of existence but more modestly the continued validity of Christianity to be the religion of intelligent man.

We have to return, therefore, to my Graham Greene account of the human situation and modify it significantly. We have to say that as the man stands there with his back to the wall of the cave, looking out towards the daylight, wondering who he is, and how he came to be there, and what is the nature of the world beyond the opening, there comes into his mind some of the things that he was taught in his childhood—that there is a Creator called God, who is his Father in heaven, that he and all men are alienated from God, that God has revealed himself in the world of nature and in the Bible, that he is most fully revealed in the man Jesus of Nazareth, that the death of this man Jesus is a redemptive death, whereby all men can be reconciled to God, and that in reconciliation to God is to be found the answer to all man's aspiration. That is the faith which I want to re-appraise, in the setting of the human situation and in the light of the considerations which the present state of human knowledge, as far as I am in a position to apprehend them, may bring to bear upon it. My hope is that I will find some answers that will, at least in part, satisfy myself, and also that I may give an example of attempting to see the christian religion 'In the Light of the Whole',[8] an example, which others better equipped than I, may emulate with very much greater success. But for myself, it is a task that can no longer be delayed.

[8] The phrase is taken from F. S. C. Northrop's essay 'In the Light of the Whole; the Present Context and Character of the World's Religions' in the *Graduate Journal*, University of Texas, Vol. VII, 1966 Supplement, pp. 47–63. The volume is given over to reporting the Gallahue Conference on World Religion held at Princeton in 1964.

Chapter Two

A PLACE OF UNDERSTANDING

MAN stands on a shrinking planet, in an expanding universe. He tries to make sense of his situation, and finds that there are two fundamental questions: who am I? and, is there anybody there? He stands and seeks to understand.

It was natural that in the early days of his self-awareness man should have answered his 'questions of ultimate concern' by the use of myths, that is (in this context) narratives which personalised the initiatives inherent in their account of man's situation. Personal actions were the only source recognised by primitive man for any initiative, so in his explanation of his world, processes were personalised and super-persons were posited to account for the on-going life of the universe. Thus the question 'who am I?', for example, gave rise to various myths which conveyed the answers: 'The gods mated and you are their offspring', or 'The gods required servants and created you to serve them', or, falling back on divine inscrutability, 'God said, Let us make man in our own image'. In every instance, the myths assured man that he was the direct result of divine creativity, a particular and very special creature, with very special privileges, the servant, ally, favourite of the powers that be.

It seems hardly possible that it is only within the last century that the resulting self-assurance was seriously challenged and indeed effectively discredited.[1] Darwin had his distinguished fore-runners with regard to the inter-relation of species even so far back as Aristotle, and more recently Linnaeus and Lamarck, but it was he who by his accumulation of the evidence established the idea of the evolution of all life from a single source by means of natural selection, and thereby placed man very firmly in his environment as the product, not of direct and personal divine activity, but of natural causes. Since his day the evidence has continued to mount. Illustrating the way in which all living organisms continue to display a basic, common pattern, George Wald has written: 'Another closely related protein is cytochrome C, one of the enzymes concerned with cellular respiration and found in all aerobic cells. This is a single chain of about 104 amino acids in a precise sequence and hence is determined by a gene containing about 312 nucleotides in sequence. Between man and the rhesus monkey, one amino acid in the chain of 104 has changed; between man and horse 12 have changed, between man and chicken 14, between man and the tuna fish 22, and between man and the yeast cell 43. The great bulk of such species-to-species changes in amino acid sequence, perhaps all of them involve changes in only one of a triplet of nucleotides. What this is saying therefore is that as between the cytochrome C. of the rhesus monkey and man, only one nucleotide has changed in 312; and as between yeast and man, only 43 nucleotides have changed out of 312.

[1] There were indeed sceptics long before the nineteenth century—the line goes back through men like Laplace and Voltaire to at least the time of Celsus and Lucian in the early christian centuries, and indeed there was a deep-seated cynicism with regard to the values of human existence in the ancient pre-christian world. Cf. the biblical Ecclesiastes (ca. 4th century BC), and from Babylon 'A Dialogue About Human Misery', ca. 1000 BC, and from Egypt 'A Dispute over Suicide', ca. 2000 BC; (*Ancient Near Eastern Texts*, ed. James Pritchard, second edit., Princeton, 1955, pp. 348 ff. and 405 ff.) But even so, the creationist view (with its in-built comforting re-assurances) prevailed overwhelmingly in western culture until Darwin produced the evidence for the naturalist view in the mid-nineteenth century.

(This is somewhat of an oversimplification, since when so many changes have occurred, some of them have occurred more than once, but this hardly changes the argument.) There was a time ages ago—perhaps one billion years, perhaps longer—in which yeast and man shared a common ancestor. Some of those ancestors went one way, eventually to become yeasts, some of the others took another road and eventually became men. Two pathways lead from that remote point at which we and yeast were one; and that double journey has resulted in a total change of 43 nucleotides out of 312. . . . None of us had ever dreamed before that such intimate relationships hold together the entire world of living organisms—that with such vast stretches of evolution coming between, we still retain so close a genetic relationship with yeast. That is a surprise, and I for one am proud of it; but proud or not, the relationship cuts very deep indeed, and once it is pointed out, it ceases to be a surprise, for it is telling us a deep and moving truth; to wit, that we are much more like yeast than we are unlike it.'[2] There can indeed no longer be any argument on the matter. Man is the result of the same natural forces as the horse, the sparrow and the potato; he is bound up in the one bundle of life with the dolphin and the shark and the prolific plankton that makes a sea phosphorescent under a tropic moon.

We cannot, in actual fact, however, trace his ancestry very far back, but in view of his obvious physiological, indeed, biochemical kinships, this is more annoying and somewhat humiliating rather than very significant. In a paper entitled 'The Crucial Evidence for Human Evolution', Sir Wilfrid Le Gros Clark summed up the pertinent data available in 1959. He pointed out that today man is represented by a single species,

[2] 'Determinacy, Individuality, and the Problem of Free Will', in *New Views of the Nature of Man*, ed. John R. Platt, Chicago, 1965, pp. 28–29. George Wald is Professor of Biology at Harvard and was recently named a Nobel prize winner.

homo sapiens. The Magdalenians (such as those who inhabited the caves of Lascaux), were anatomically identical with modern Europeans, and their remains date back to the later phases of the last of the Pleistocene glaciations, that is some fifteen thousand to twenty thousand years ago. The remains associated with the earlier Aurignacian culture give a radioactive carbon dating of twenty-seven thousand years. At Florisbad in South Africa a skull attributed to *homo sapiens* gave a carbon dating of forty thousand years. The Early Mousterians, a more primitive type of man extant in Europe in the latter part of the last inter-glacial period, seem to have been the ancestors of both *homo sapiens* and *homo neanderthalensis*. The former seems to have displaced the latter, who was a cousin, rather than an ancestor of *homo sapiens*, and a distinctly less intelligent species. At any rate, the Neanderthals were somewhat later than the Mousterians but gave way quite suddenly to *homo sapiens*. When we reach back into the Middle Pleistocene we have evidence of the widespread distribution in Africa, Asia and Europe of a still more primitive type of hominid, which has been recognised as a separate genus and named *pithecanthropos*, or ape-man. His remains have been found, for example, near Peking and in Java, and also in Algeria and possibly near Heidleberg, though the problem of correctly identifying and classifying this kind of material gives plenty of scope for argument among the experts. The discoveries since 1924 in the Transvaal in South Africa have provided evidence of what would seem to be an even more primitive but still distinctly hominid creature dating back to the Early Pleistocene period, that is possibly a million years ago. The somewhat unfortunate name *australopithecus* or 'southern ape' was given to this creature but he certainly deserves his place in the ancestral tree of our species. There, however, the present line of evidence peters out. Professor Clark sums his survey up as follows: 'We have now traced in retrospect a graded morphological series, arranged in an ordered time sequence, linking *homo sapiens* through Early Mousterian man, pre-Mousterian man, and the small-brained *pithecanthropus*, with the still smaller-brained *australopithecus*. This sequence comprises a remarkable confirmation of the connecting links postulated and predicted by Darwin's hypothesis of the descent of man, at any rate as far back as the Early Pleistocene. There is no conspicuous gap in the sequence, but there remains a serious gap covering the preceding period of the Pliocene. We know that, during the early part of the Pliocene, and throughout the Miocene period before then, many interesting varieties of anthropoid apes were distributed over wide areas of the Old World, in Europe, Asia and Africa. It is also the case that some of these fossil apes show generalised features of the skull, dentition and limb bones which might well have provided the structural basis for the subsequent emergence and differentiation of the hominid line of evolution. But as yet we have no objective evidence to show just when or how, the emergence of this new line took place.'[3]

If then we cannot trace the evolutionary development of man with the same detail and with the same continuity as we can that of the horse or the dog, at least we have more than enough evidence to give a confident first answer to the questions of ultimate concern 'Who am I, where did I come from?'. That answer is: 'I came out of the long incredibly complex process which we all too glibly call "evolution".' But the fact that we are here, in this world, and above all able to ask this question, emphasises that that answer is an amazing one, even more so than that of the direct-creationist theory. When we consider the ascent of man through the long passages of evolution, the blind alleys unchosen (I am thinking, for

[3] 'The Crucial Evidence for Human Evolution', *Proceedings*, The American Philosophical Society, Vol. 103 (1959), No. 2, pp. 159–172. Sir Wilfrid Le Gros Clark was Professor of Anatomy at Oxford.

example, of 'old four-legs', the *coelacanth*, which settled into unchanging stability seventy or more million years ago)[4] and wrong turnings retraced (I am thinking of *homo neanderthalensis*), we contemplate a matter of great wonder, and if we have any imagination at all, we renew our sense of the mystery of our being, and echo the psalmist: 'I am fearfully and wonderfully made.'[5] The concept of evolution, so far from having banished awe from the world, has replenished man's sense of wonder, as the old creationist myths long ceased to do. But who am I?

The question still remains largely unanswered. If I am the end-product (so far) of this truly remarkable process, what kind of a being am I? Clearly, I am an animal, blood-brother to the other animals and indeed to every other form of life that has appeared upon this planet. In comparison with my fellow-animals, at least, I am very intelligent, having a brain-case of from 900 cc. to 2,300 cc., whereas the most the anthropoid apes have ever recorded is 685 cc.—though whether the size of the brain-case is all that important is in some doubt; the important fact appears to be the brain's refinement of organisation. In fact there is still a very great deal about myself that I do not know, and I have to admit that I am my own greatest enigma. This is particularly true when I come to consider myself as an individual, which I now have to do.

[4] Cf. the interesting account of the re-discovery of this fish, thought to be long extinct, in *Old Four Legs: The Story of the Coelacanth*, J. L. B. Smith, London, 1956.

[5] So many of the best things in the King James Version are doubtful translations. The Hebrew at Psalm 139:13 reads: 'I praise thee because wonderful things I am wonderful. Wonderful things are thy works.' This is almost certainly a corrupt text and RSV amends to 'I praise thee for thou art fearful and wonderful. Wonderful are thy works,' which is probably as good a guess at the original as we can make. The Jerusalem Bible paraphrases: 'for all these mysteries, I thank you: for the wonder of myself, for the wonder of your works.' Whether all that can be obtained from the Hebrew I am very doubtful; but that all that and more is our intelligent response to the concept of evolution I am in no doubt whatsoever.

The physiological account of the individual man is in its main outlines fairly well determined. The creature is a very complex organism, the proper functioning of which is maintained by a supply of materials which in many cases have to be pre-processed by other living organisms before this particular creature can assimilate them—for example, it cannot by itself produce protein from inorganic matter. Its metabolic processes are extremely intricate, and depend upon the presence of a very large number of enzymes, or ferments in the digestive juices which render food substances soluble and diffusible. Without them (and they run into many hundreds, even thousands) the body cannot properly function. The biochemistry of the reproductive process is only now, since the work of O. T. Avery in the middle forties, beginning to be discernable in any detail, but the 'breaking' of the 'genetic code' was one of the greatest achievements of science. Once produced, the individual begins to function after the manner of his species and his 'behaviour',[6] despite tantalising lacunae in the presently available description, is now fairly well accounted for: a stimulus is received by the sensory nerves with which the body is generously equipped; these stimuli set up biochemical processes which result in electrical pulses being carried along the nerve-system to the cortex of the brain, where there is an interchange of sensory and motor impulses; from the cortex an electrical pulse is transmitted by the motor nerves to the requisite muscle and the 'behaviour' results.

This greatly simplified account, however, suffers from the great weakness that it allows the conclusion that any individual's

---

[6] *'Behaviour* is the publicly observable activity of muscles or glands of external excretion as manifested in movements of parts of the body or in the appearance of tears, sweat, saliva and so forth. Talking is behaviour; so is a smile, a grimace, eye-watering, trembling, blushing (which is produced by muscular changes in blood vessels), changing one's posture or following the words of a printed page with one's eyes.' D. O. Hebb, *A Textbook of Psychology*, Philadelphia and London, 1958, p. 2.

behaviour should, if the appropriate data is fully known, be wholly and mechanistically predictable. Yet the creature—'I'— has the ineradicable conviction that in at least some small areas of his existence he exercises choice: that is, he has a measure of free-will. He conceives of himself as a 'personality', and as having a 'mind' which is something other than merely physiological processes. The problem, then, is to know whether this is sheer delusion, or whether it can be taken into the intelligent account of man (I do not say 'scientific account' for in this context that is itself a question-begging term) and made a part of the answer to the basic question 'Who am I?'. It is in order to deal with that problem that behaviouristic psychology has set itself the task of attempting a description of man which will fully account for his behaviour without invoking any concept of consciousness, mind, soul, personality or the like, other than is demanded by scientifically-observable phenomena. The proviso, as we shall see, is important.

It is now possible, owing to the physiological and psychological advances of the past two or three decades, to set the problem out quite clearly, and few scientists have done this so effectively as my colleague Professor Donald Hebb. In his book *The Organisation of Behaviour*, he writes: 'Modern psychology takes completely for granted that behaviour and neural function are perfectly correlated, that one is completely caused by the other. There is no soul or life-force to stick a finger into the brain now and then and make neural cells do what they would not otherwise. . . . One cannot be a determinist in physics and chemistry and biology, and a mystic in psychology.' He continues: 'The central problem with which we must find a way to deal can be put in two different ways. Psychologically, it is the problem of thought: some sort of process that is not fully controlled by environmental stimulation and yet co-operates closely with that stimulation. From another point of view, physiologically, the problem is that of the transmission of excitation from sensory to motor cortex. ... The failure of psychology to handle thought adequately (or the failure of neurophysiology to tell us how to conceive of cortical transmission) has been the essential weakness of modern psychological theory. ...'[7] Here then is the problem. As an animal,[8] that is a physiologically-describable organism, man's behaviour should be wholly explicable in neurophysiological terms: the activating stimulus operates upon the sensory nerves which convey the signal to the cortex where an exchange of excitation between the afferent cells and the efferent cells passes the signal to the motor nerves and the responsive action of muscle, organ, limb results. But there is another phenomenon that has to be taken into account. Psychologists have recognised, as Professor Hebb points out, that it is as much an observable fact as any other that response to stimulus is often not immediate but is delayed until some process of selection of behaviour has taken place. 'In the simplest terms "attention" refers to a selectivity of response. Man or animal is continuously responding to some events in the environment and not to others that could be responded to (or "noticed") just as well. When an experimental result makes it necessary to refer to "set" or "attention", the reference means, precisely, that the activity that controls the form, speed, strength, or duration of response is not the immediately preceding excitation of receptor cells alone. The fact that a response is not so controlled may be

[7] *The Organisation of Behaviour*, A Neurophysical Theory, D. O. Hebb, New York and London, 1949. The quotations in the text are from the Introduction, pp. xiii and xvi.

[8] Professor Hebb is careful to point out that the problem is not in fact confined to its relevance to man: 'In mammals even as low as the rat it has turned out to be impossible to describe behaviour as an interaction directly between sensory and motor processes. Something like *thinking* that is, intervenes. 'Thought' undoubtedly has the connotation of a human degree of complexity in cerebral function and may mean too much to be applied to lower animals. But even in the rat there is evidence that behaviour is not completely controlled by immediate sensory events: there are central processes operating also.' Ibid. p. xvi.

hard to explain, theoretically, but it is not mystical, and "attention" is not necessarily anthropomorphic, or animistic, or undefinable.' Dr Hebb comments 'the tradition in psychology has long been a search for the property in the stimulus which by itself determines the ensuing response, at any given stage of learning. This approach seems partly a consequence of psychology's persistent fight against animism and deserves respect for that reason; but it is no longer satisfactory as a theory'.[9]

It is important to recognise that Professor Hebb rejects 'the assumption of a complete sensory control' (that is, that the individual is wholly activated by the stimulus operating upon him), only because it does not adequately explain the facts of behaviour. His study is always objective and in terms of scientifically-describable phenomena—movement, physiological change, neuroelectrical activity of the cortex, and the like. This must be unreservedly accepted by any intelligent person as a truly proper and thoroughly commendable proceeding. Given the physiological facts now at our command, we can do no other. The physical basis of personality has been known to us at least since the time of William Lawrence's *Lectures on Comparative Anatomy*, an annual series delivered to the Royal College of Surgeons in the years 1816–1818, and published in 1819. As June Goodfield-Toulmin points out, Lawrence very effectively raised the question 'what in a word, is "life"?', and she continues: 'In the early years of the nineteenth century we find several different forms of answer to this question. Here I am concerned only with two. First, the doctrine that life was "a principle superadded to matter" and secondly, the theory that life results both from the very organisation of living matter, and the action of mutually interdependent processes. The first view was placed firmly into biological circulation by John Hunter. The second view, even if it did not originate with William Lawrence, found in him one of its most eloquent exponents, and is

[9] *Op. cit.* p. 4.

clearly coming into its own in the second half of the twentieth century.'[10] Surely, Dr Toulmin is too cautious in her last remark; for any intelligent person who has become even generally aware of the accumulation of evidence from virology, cytology, genetics, pharmacology and the new interdisciplinary studies that go under the name of 'molecular biology', the agreement of the testimony is quite conclusive.[11] Life, we may confidently affirm, is a phenomenon which results from the organisation of matter. But this is not to say that the enigma 'what, in a word, is life' has been answered. Life may be a phenomenon dependent on matter but nevertheless it is clearly not identifiable with matter, and its essential nature still remains to be grasped. As Willard Libby remarks, 'life apparently is natural in the sense that all the ingredients except the final magic seem to be present naturally'.[12] It is that 'final magic' which still eludes us.

The psychologists are, however, clearly right in their assertion that our explanation of 'behaviour' must be pushed as far as possible in neurophysiological terms. But it is equally clear, at

[10] 'Blasphemy and Biology', in *The Rockefeller University Review*, September–October, 1966, pp. 9–18. June Goodfield-Toulmin is Professor of the History and Philosophy of Science at Wellesley College.

[11] Cf. for example the Penguin volume *The Physical Basis of Personality* London, 1944 by V. H. Mottram, formerly Professor of Physiology in the University of London. Some at least of the effects of the so-called 'psychedelic' drugs are becoming a matter of public knowledge and indeed of public concern.

[12] Cf. 'Man's Place in the Physical Universe', *New Views of the Nature of Man*, ed. John R. Platt, Chicago, 1965, p. 1. Cf. also p. 5; 'All in all, there is little difficulty in seeing that the early conditions that probably developed on earth would support life, and that these conditions evolved naturally as part of the whole machinery of planetary and atmospheric formation. At the same time, few scientists have had the temerity to attempt to explain the magical transition from the inanimate to the animate in a scientific way . . . I think that now, as we are coming to understand how the whole stage can be nicely set for the waving of the life-giving wand and the occurrence of the miracle (or however you will describe it), many of us wait with bated breath for some further understanding of how it happened.' Professor Libby, a Nobel prize winner for his work in radiocarbon dating, is Director of the Institute of Geophysics, at the University of California at Los Angeles.

least to myself, that a purely physiological answer to the question 'who am I?' will never be wholly satisfactory. 'The product of evolution, a member of the species *homo sapiens*, a creature exhibiting as a result of the complex organisation of its physical structures the phenomenon called "life"' is the answer we have so far arrived at, and it is not enough. It is not enough because, as Professor Hebb pointed out with regard to the earlier, simple model of the behavioural-psychological theory, it does not deal with all the facts. So, too, any theory which attempts to deal with life in purely physiological terms will be judged inadequate, because there is a whole range of human experience for which it does not account.

The first such experiences are those which centre in 'self-awareness'. 'I' may be an animated telephone-exchange but the exchange has the very curious (and incidentally quite un-mechanistic) ability to be aware of itself. I cannot ignore the fact that I am writing these words on this paper—a very publicly observable form of 'behaviour'—because 'I' am thinking these thoughts. Surely Descartes was indisputably right when he said that 'I' cannot doubt that 'I' exist: *Cogito ergo sum*. This self-awareness is in fact the most basic feature of man's mental existence.[13]

Moreover, this sense of my own being is so strong that when I recognise it in another, I immediately sense a different relationship with that other. In Martin Buber's famous phrase, I am aware of an 'I-thou' relationship which is quite different from an 'I-it' relationship. Self-awareness is thus a major fact of everyday experience and any attempt to answer the

[13] Cf. Teilhard de Chardin in 'A Summary of my Phenomenological Perspective on the World': 'As a result of some "hominising" cerebral mutation taking place among the Anthropoids towards the end of the Tertiary period, psychic Reflection, which is not only *knowing* but *knowing that one knows*, makes its irruption into the World and opens an entirely new domain to Evolution', cited *Teilhard de Chardin, the Man and his Thought*, p. 168 (Paris edit. 1961), (cf. note 7 on p. 25).

question 'Who am I' has to deal adequately with it. It is quite legitimate to withstart observable 'behaviour' and to push the enquiry as far as one can with such data. It is also quite legitimate to argue that *within the discipline as so delimited* animistic theories have to be shunned like the devil. But it is quite false to say that no other enquiry may not take the positive results of the behaviouristic enquiry and add to these the considerations which arise out of man's undeniable sense of self-awareness and then ask what concept of man emerges from the larger enquiry. Indeed, unless I do this, I cannot ask the question 'Who am I?'—and I do ask it. I have to ask it. I cannot cease, every day, from facing that question in a thousand ways: 'Who am I?' That is one of the things which the existentialist philosophers have made very clear. And the philosopher has a right to be heard as well as the psychologist.

Another range of experiences which have to be taken into account is that of free-will. The great interest of Professor Wald's paper, previously cited, is that it seeks on a purely physiological basis to give an account of free will. He writes: 'through the factors we have been discussing, the complexity of the organism, its dynamic state, and the constant intrusion of genetic disorder, one can be quite convinced that each living thing, including each living man, is unique, an individual unlike any other in space or time. But to those factors one must add another of ultimate importance. It is that living organisms store history. Not only does each of us come into the world with a unique composition and inheritance but to those we begin to accumulate a unique experience. That personal history, growing throughout our lives, is ours alone. That private self that is you or I is the unique composition and structure that come to us via metabolism and inheritance, coupled with a unique personal history that is for ever growing. . . . When the time comes to make a decision, to exercise what we call free will, to choose—when that time comes, the self that exercises free will is, I think, that unique private self, that unique product of the unique composition, genetics and history, all to a degree unknown. At that moment, no one can predict the outcome, neither an outsider nor the person making the decision, because no one has the requisite information. So I should say that the essence of free will is not a failure of determinism but a failure of predictability.'[14] This is fine, but not fine enough. From the physiological point of view it goes as far as anyone can go— and incidentally ends with a splendid call for us to defend stoutly against political and social encroachment the limited area of free will which remains to us—but I do not find it adequate to explain my own sense of a limited but nevertheless real freedom of choice in a great many situations which concern my everyday living. To be told that my molecules determine my every choice reduces my wrestlings with conscience, or my agonising over truly important decisions—whether to emigrate to Canada or not, for example—to a mere play-acting. To believe this would make life quite unlivable. In a single day I am called upon to vote for or against the promotion of a colleague to full professorship; I am asked whether I will or will not travel six hundred miles in six months' time to address a conference; I am consulted by my wife on the colour of the new living-room carpet; I am asked whether I want the fish or the meat course at dinner; whether I want to listen to a recording of Bach's 'Musical Offering' or of 'The Sound of Music'. My self-respect depends very largely on the degree of seriousness which I accord to these varying matters. To believe that in fact I have no choice, and that it is irrelevant that I give my full and very careful attention to some matters, and merely throw off an indifferent answer to others, would undermine the integrity of my personal relationships and completely destroy my self-respect. A man must take his major

[14] 'Determinacy, Individuality, and the Problem of Free Will', *op. cit.* pp. 33 and 37 (cf. note 2, p. 31).

judgements seriously or disintegrate. In one sense that is what existentialism is all about.

A third range of experiences which have to come into our reckoning are those connected with the idea of value. Traditionally these have been categorised as goodness, truth and beauty, but they shade off into each other as Keats recognised in his line 'Beauty is truth, truth beauty—that is all Ye know on earth, and all ye need to know', and as the Fourth Evangelist saw when he made right action the basis for right judgement.[15] Probably all sense of values springs originally from the need to recognise the difference between fact and unfact. To say 'there is no tiger in that cave' when in fact there is a tiger in the cave, is a matter of life and death. To realise that two and two make four is to grasp a fundamental lesson: that two and two are four and no amount of fantasy or myth or magic will make them otherwise. It is a recognition of the givenness of the universe in which we live, and that we had better recognise it or we will not live in it very long. Truth is indeed a precious commodity. Facts were sacred, long before C. P. Scott delivered his aphorism. Similarly, the moral sense may well have a factual origin. Because the sense of self-awareness and its concomitant conviction of free-will is so strong within him, a man who meets another being giving evidence of that same self-awareness, and that same conviction of free-will, recognises that here is a being inherently different from all the rest of nature, which does not possess this characteristic. Free-will gives a power to initiate which beings not possessing this quality do not have. Those that do possess it have therefore to be treated with more circumspection. Chairs can be pushed around, but not people. Not to recognise that has often had bad consequences individually and socially. It is a fundamental error to treat persons as things, and whenever the human judgement, individual or collective, recognises that this is being done, there is protest

[15] John 7:17.

and outcry. This is what gives rise to trade-unionism, civil rights programmes, and all the varied protest movements of our day. A man 'ought' to treat other men as men; and with this recognition the sense of morality is born. As for beauty, it is possibly the child of the marriage of truth and goodness. It is a derived value. When something is manifestly true (that is, coherent with its context) and obviously right (that is, making an appeal to our sense of what is moral) it challenges us to be more of a person in order to comprehend it. Thus it flatters us, encourages us, we think well of it, we find it pleasing and appropriate. In that moment beauty detaches herself from her parents and stands independent and fully one in this trinity of man's perceptiveness. That may be a possible explanation of the origin of the sense of beauty. At any rate, however established, these values go on to develop, to broaden in scope, to arouse emotion and to evoke very strong loyalties. They are certainly categories which influence our judgement a thousand times each day.

Self-awareness, the sense of free-will, the sense of values, these are a quite different series of phenomena from those with which the behaviourist psychologist chooses to work. Nevertheless they are as much facts of human existence as are 'the publicly observable activity of muscles or glands of external excretion'. When we set out to answer the question 'Who am I?', these matters have to be taken into account, just as fully as the findings of the neurologists and the physiologists. Our problem is to construct a hypothesis which will do justice both to the findings of the behavioural scientists, and to the self-awareness, the sense of freedom of choice, and the sense of values by which men live.

Let us return to Professor Hebb. He has advanced a theory which has commended itself widely to fellow psychologists, and which I attempt to take into my own thinking. Since, however, I am under obligation not to misrepresent a colleague,

I add his own summary of his theory in a footnote.[16] The stimulus excites the sensory nerves and the impulse is transmitted to the cortex of the brain, where it activates many other cells. It is suggested that a series of identical or near-identical stimuli can set up in the cortex a pattern of cells, acting as a closed circuit which will constitute a 'holding' pattern, or memory. Such a pattern may excite other patterns and a sequence of such excitations may be the 'thought-process. Moreover, the cortex acts in some way the physiologists have not yet explained as a memory bank. Dr Wilder Penfield has

---

[16] *The Organisation of Behaviour*, pp. xviii-xix: 'In the chapters that follow this introduction I have tried to lay a foundation for such a theory. It is, on the one hand and from the physiologist's point of view, quite speculative. On the other hand, it achieves some synthesis of psychological knowledge, and it attempts to hold as strictly as possible to the psychological evidence in those long stretches where the guidance of anatomy and physiology is lacking. The desideratum is a conceptual tool for dealing with expectancy, attention, and so on, and with a temporally organised intracerebral process. But this would have little value if it did not also comprise the main facts of perception, and of learning. To achieve something of the kind, the limitations of a scheme are accepted with the purpose of developing certain conceptions of neural action. In outline, the conceptual structure is as follows: Any frequently repeated, particular stimulation will lead to the slow development of a "cell assembly", a diffuse structure comprising cells in the cortex and diencephalon (and also, perhaps, in the basal ganglia of the cerebrum), capable of acting briefly as a closed system, delivering facilitation to other such systems and usually having a specific motor facilitation. A series of such events constitutes a "phase sequence"—the thought process. Each assembly action may be aroused by a preceding assembly, by a sensory event, or—normally—by both. The central facilitation from one of these activities on the next is the prototype of "attention". The theory proposes that in this central facilitation, and its varied relationship to sensory processes, lies the answer to an issue that is made inescapable by Humphrey's (1940) penetrating review of the problem of the direction of thought.

The kind of cortical organisation discussed in the preceding paragraph is what is regarded as essential to adult waking behaviour. It is proposed also that there is an alternate, 'intrinsic' organisation, occurring in sleep and in infancy, which consists of hypersynchrony in the firing of cortical cells. But besides these two forms of cortical organisation, there may be disorganisation. It is assumed that the assembly depends completely on a very delicate timing which might be disturbed by metabolic changes as well as by sensory events that do not accord with the pre-existent central process. When this is transient, it is called emotional disturbance; when chronic, neurosis or psychosis.'

demonstrated that an artificial stimulation of certain areas of the cortex can evoke for the patient memories, some of which he had long since forgotten.[17] The cortex is continuously throughout the whole of the individual's life in a state of excitement; indeed a more scientific test for death than heart-stopping is the remaining steady at zero of the electroence-phalagram, or reading of the electrical discharge of the cortex. So then, when a stimulus is received it may provoke an immediate motor-reaction, as when one's hand inadvertently touches a hot-plate, or it may be subjected to the thought-process as when one hears a remark and ponders a reply. The body reserves the operation of this second process for 'non-vital' matters—we react as we say 'instinctively' to bodily harm or threatening physical danger, and the thought-process is not normally allowed to interfere with matters like the beating of the heart or the drawing of breath. Professor Wald[18] tells how Francis Galton forced his thought-process to take over the control of his breathing one day, only breathing when he thought to do so, but was over-successful, since when he wanted to remit the matter again to automatic control he was unable to do so, and for a bad half-hour he nearly suffocated. This all suggests (what indeed must from other considerations be the case) that thought is a late biological development and has only a limited rôle to play in the successful existence of the individual of the species *homo sapiens*. For the most part the body functions more or less automatically on a stimulus-response pattern.

So far we have respected the competence of the behaviourist psychologist.[19] But now we need to go further and take into

[17] Dr Penfield was Professor of Neurology and Neurosurgery at McGill, and Director of the Montreal Neurological Institute. Cf. *Epilepsy and the Functional Anatomy of the Human Brain*, Wilder Penfield and Herbert Jasper, Boston, 1954, pp. 126–147.

[18] He refers to Galton's *Memories of My Life*, London, 1908, p. 276.

[19] It is important to recognise how immensely significant is the work of Professor Hebb and his colleagues in experimental psychology. They have effected a truly Copernican revolution on such subjects as perception,

account that introspective evidence which the behaviourist psychologist by a disciplinary decision very properly excludes from his data. The area of existence given over to the thought-process may be very limited, but it is nevertheless the most important part of the individual's life. His thoughts, his hopes, his fears, his considered judgments, his agonised decisions and his intellectual enjoyments, are for him the truly significant part of his being alive.

We have, therefore, to extend the behaviourist-psychologist's model something after this manner: the cortex builds up its patterns and stores its memory-banks, and the thought-process is set in operation. Once started, however, it begins to develop in an independent fashion. The various patterns and memories are related to each other in a unifying way, so that an organised, intellectual 'entity' is formed out of a mass of related thought-patterns and memory circuits, the relation being in fact the history of the organism: we are each one of us a series of memory-circuit contents and thought-patterns strung on a thread of unique experience or personal history. This 'entity' then performs the astonishing feat on which everything else depends: it thinks of itself. We may conceive that this is done, as it were, in two stages. The biological organism is aware of an object, let us say a tree. After experience of many trees, the patterns of memory in the cortex, build a general 'tree' pattern—i.e. the brain has conceived the idea of a tree, as opposed to either the contemporary experience of a particular tree, or the stored-experience (i.e. memory) of many trees.

---

learning and memory, and in so doing have completely out-dated the philosophical discussion of epistemology from Descartes through to Russell. Any discussion of the subject which does not start from an account of the physiological facts is now irrelevant. Yet the able and lively article on 'The Theory of Knowledge' in the current edition of the *Encyclopedia Britannica* by Professor A. D. Woozley of St Andrews can still discuss the subject of perception as if the work of the behaviourists had not been begun. (*Encyclopedia Britannica*, 1967, Vol. 13, pp. 419–432. The naive references to psychology on p. 420 only serve to emphasize the point.)

The brain has reached the level of being able to construct a pattern of its own, that is a mental concept. This, however, is a cortical activity which is wholly initiated within the cortex and is independent of outside stimuli. Its occurrence is the moment of deliverance from biological determinism. The second stage is where the mind—for we have now transcended (but not escaped) the brain—relates this ability to create a mental concept (i.e. a cortical pattern) of external objects to itself; based on memory patterns of its personal history, it builds a new cortical pattern of its own experience of itself, thus taking the step which confers incipient humanity, whereby the entity says 'I am'.

Some such hypothesis gains considerable support from the writings of Roger Sperry. He says, for example, in his essay 'Mind, Brain and Humanist Values', 'One can still find here and there in the literature a modicum of some final, perhaps "last rite", respect paid to the psyche. For example, there is the acceptance by Charles Sherrington of the possible co-existence of two separate phenomenal realms in the brain, and there is the stand of Carl Rogers that man's inner experience must be recognised as well as the brain mechanism of objective psychology. In the existence of two such very different realms, Rogers sees a lasting paradox with which we all must learn to live. But even the dualists are quite prepared to go along these days with the conviction held by most brain researchers—up to some 99.9 per cent of us, I suppose—that conscious mental forces can be safely ignored, insofar as the objective, scientific study of the brain is concerned. In the pages that follow, I am going to line myself up with the 0.1 per cent or so mentalist minority in a stand that admittedly also goes well beyond the facts. It is a position, however, that seems to me equally strong and somewhat more appealing than those we have just outlined. In my own hypothetical brain model, conscious awareness does get representation as a very real causal agent and rates an important place in the causal sequence and chain of control in brain events, in which it appears as an active, operational force. Any model or description that leaves out conscious forces, according to this view, is bound to be sadly incomplete and unsatisfactory. The conscious mind in this scheme, far from being put aside as a by-product, epiphenomenon, or inner aspect, is located front and centre, directly in the midst of the causal interplay of cerebral mechanisms. Mind and consciousness are put in the driver's seat, as it were: they give the orders, and they push and haul around the physiology and the physical and chemical processes as much as or more than the latter processes direct them. This scheme is one that puts mind back over matter, in a sense, not under or outside or beside it. It is a scheme that idealizes ideas and ideals over physical and chemical interactions, nerve impulse traffic and DNA. It is a brain model in which conscious mental psychic forces are recognised to be the crowning achievement of some five hundred million years or more of evolution.'[20]

[20] In *New Views of Man*, ed. John R. Platt, Chicago, 1965, pp. 77–78. Roger W. Sperry is Professor of Psychobiology at the California Institute of Technology. Cf. further pp. 78, 79, 82: 'Now, what is the argument in favour of mentalism, the argument that holds that ideas and other mental entities push around the physiological and biochemical events in the brain? The argument is simple and goes as follows: First, it contends that mind and consciousness are dynamic, emergent (pattern or configurational) properties of the living brain in action. There are usually plenty of "takers" on this first point, including even some of the tough-minded brain researchers, as, for example, the outstanding neuroanatomist, C. J. Herrick. Second, the argument goes a critical step farther and insists that these emergent properties in the brain have causal potency—just as they do elsewhere in the universe.... In other words, the flow and the timing of impulse traffic through any brain cell, or even a nucleus of cells in the brain, are governed largely by the over-all encompassing properties of the whole cerebral circuit system, within which the given cells and fibers are incorporated, and also by the relationship of this circuit system to other circuit systems. Further, the dynamic properties of the cerebral system as a whole, and the way in which these properties direct and govern the flow of impulse traffic throughout the system— that is, the general circuit properties of the whole brain—may undergo radical and widespread changes from one moment to the next with just the flick of a cerebral facilitatory "set". This set is a shifting pattern of central

The behaviourist psychologist may protest and say that we have thereby retreated to animism, but the facts must be allowed to dictate the theory and not *vice versa*. It is a fact that I think, I hope, I purpose and I decide, and no amount of physiological or behaviourist theory can be allowed to negate that phenomenon. I cannot come to terms with myself unless at some point I can break the tyranny of the cortex. But if I understand that my self-awareness, my mind, emanates from the cortex, and is biologically dependent for its existence upon the cortex, but nevertheless achieves a limited, but most precious mental independence from the cortex, then, and only then, I can be a man.

That area of freedom may be very small, but if it exists at all it is enough. When Naaman, the leper cured by Elisha the prophet of Yahweh, was returning to his own land, the land of the god Rimmon, he asked for two mule-loads of Yahweh's earth, that he might spread it in his courtyard and thereon lay his prayer-mat, and so have a *locus standi* before Yahweh.[21] So, too, I must have my small area of freedom of thought and freedom of will, or 'I' cannot stand anywhere.

'Who am I'? I am the product of evolution. I am the descendent of hominoid apes, of hominids, of *australopithecus*,

---

excitation that will open or prime one group of circuit pathways with its own special pattern properties, while at the same time closing, repressing, or inhibiting endless other circuit potentialities that might otherwise be open and available for impulse traffic. These changes of "set" are responsible, for example, for such things as a shift of attention, a turn of thought, a change of feeling, or a new insight. To make a long story short, if one keeps climbing upward in the chain of command within the brain, one finds at the very top those over-all organisational forces and dynamic properties of the large patterns of cerebral excitation that are correlated with mental states of psychic activity . . . . The central, emergent conscious force within the brain, as visualised here, is not a simple surrounding envelope, or volume property, or any other kind of "isomorph", as the Gestalt schools tried to make it. It is rather a functional pattern that has to be worked out in entirely new terms, that is, in terms of the functional circuitry of the brain, in terms of the still unknown brain code.'

[21] 2 Kings 5:15–19.

pithecanthropus, of Mousterian man, of the Aurignacians, of the Magdalenians. My culture emerged in Babylon five thousand years ago. As an individual I am a highly-evolved creature in which thought and self-consciousness, what we call 'mind', has emanated from the purely biological functioning of my cortical organism. I am 'I'—the sum total of my experiences and my memories, a unique individual because I have a unique history. Indeed, 'I' is my history. But as I stand on a shrinking planet in an expanding universe, at least I know that I am, and that I am not a thing but a person. That is my first belief-affirmation and thereafter I have to live in that faith.

Chapter Three

AN UNDERSTANDING OF GOD

THERE are two questions which we all pose to ourselves at some time or another and they are of such a fundamental nature and they differ so markedly in quality from all other questions, that they are called 'existential', as relating to man's very existence. The first we have already discussed—'Who am I?'—and now we must turn to the second—'Am I alone?'. As he stands on his shrinking planet in an expanding universe, seeking to understand his situation, these are the questions which touch upon his very existence.

The second question sounds at first quite ludicrous. In this time of population explosion, man's increasing numbers constitute by far the greatest threat to his own future, since overcrowding breeds poverty, hunger and war. In the past it could be countered by emigration, but there are now few under-populated areas. F. W. Boreham, in one of his colourful paragraphs brings home to us one of the surprising and indeed serious ecological facts relating to man—he is everywhere. 'He is a master migrant. He scorns all the limits that temperature and climate impose on other creatures. Neither polar snows nor equatorial suns deter him in his restless wanderings and incongruous settlements. He comes like a ghost upon the Arctic foxes and the Polar bears as he bursts amid their snow and ice.

He startles the elephant and the lion as he crosses the Equator. The antelope and the giraffe fly in terror before him across the veldt. The meek-eyed camel looks round at him in surprise as he sets out in its company across the desert. The sea-fowl scream around his head as he negotiates the oceans. North, south, east and west—he is everywhere.'[1] That, if we can overlook the 'meek-eyed' camel, is well said. Man has in fact swarmed all over his planet. It sounds ludicrous therefore to say that for each individual of the species, the second existential question is 'Am I alone?'.

Nevertheless this element of the ludicrous is part of the significance of the question. As he comes to self-awareness, each man finds himself demanding a relationship. He is a person, and one of the characteristics of personality is the need to be recognised and treated as a person and not as a thing. Moreover, he is not satisfied to be so regarded by his fellow men and women; he has a hunger to be treated as a person by the universe, by Life itself. One is reminded of the adolescent who, seeking companionship and being referred to the play-mates of earlier days, shrugs them off with a comprehensive dismissal: 'Oh, they don't count!'. The young adult wants to be accepted as such by other adults; it is part of his development to need to be accepted into an adult world; this is an experience in which his former friendships can no longer satisfy him. They are gratefully remembered, but now 'they don't count'. So, too, in man's existential situation, he is glad of the personal consideration and the tentative understanding which relates him meaningfully to other members of his species, but that is not what he means when he cries 'Am I alone?'. He is looking for recognition from the universe itself.

Each of us is aware of himself. He knows he is the product of natural processes and that his very self-awareness emanates from the complexity of his organismic structure. But is this

[1] 'The First Swallow' in *The Golden Milestone*, London, 1914, pp. 40–41.

53

self-awareness a freak of nature, a biological sport, something with which the universe is not geared to deal, or is it truly part of the whole process? In other words is man an outcaste, an alien in a non-personal universe, or is he the *raison d'être* of the whole process? He is like an accident victim returning to consciousness after a long coma. As he opens his eyes and focuses them inexpertly and fumblingly on this unknown environment, will he discern a face looking kindly down upon him, or has he been switched by the accident into a science-fiction world, and will find himself in an automated factory, self-servicing, self-repairing, hermetically sealed, a world of machinery into which by cruel mischance he has been somehow introduced but in which he is the only living creature? Is he alone, or is Somebody there?

The two situations I have suggested are unsatisfactory because they are question-begging, but it is doubtful whether any others we might imagine would be any less compromised and in any case they do serve to point up the question being begged. The man coming to consciousness after an accident, painfully focusing his eyes and discerning a face looking down in sympathy and friendliness accepts the personal relationship as primary, and the bed he is lying on, the room, the hospital, drugs, treatment as all subordinate to and indeed part of the person-who-is-the-face. He has the assurance that 'he is being looked after'. The man introduced into an automated factory might wander around, trying to find out how the operational system worked and for what end-product it was set up, and he might also wonder vaguely if the whole thing had an operations-research engineer, or whether at least somewhere there was a janitor. We have in fact arrived at the question as to whether there is in relation to our universe a 'God', but if we find one of these metaphors more satisfying than the other we have already begun to take sides in a vigorous debate. One of the many things that J. A. T. Robinson did in his provocative book

Honest to God was to popularise Tillich's exposition of the inadequacy of the engineer-janitor concept of God, and to argue for the 'nurse-who-is-the-face', that is, the personal character of life as a whole. Robinson's view has been caricatured as 'Not God' "up in heaven", nor God "out there", but God "down here".' His own phrase however is 'a depth at the centre of life' and this is his paraphrase of Tillich's 'the Ground of being', and I find both these phrases as very meaningful.[2] What they assert is that God is not apart from the totality but is the totality; or at least, they assert that the negative part of that sentence is true, even if we are not sure how to phrase the positive.

In other words, the classic question 'Is there a God?' is no longer meaningful. The form of the question makes him one entity among others, as if there were trees and mountains and electricity and animals and weather and God. The answer is in fact supplied by what you put into the word 'God'. If you mean a Divine Being, other than and conceivable apart from, the universe of our experience (in effect what I have termed the 'engineer-janitor' concept) the answer is surely 'no'. Such a concept is the classic case of explaining the known, the universe, by the unknown, God. It multiplies entities unnecessarily. It is an untidy hypothesis to account for the undoubted existence of the universe and Laplace was thoroughly sound when he told Napoleon that it was a hypothesis of which he had no need. If, however, by 'God' you mean that life, the totality of the universe, has in it a personal dimension to which the personal in my being is sensitive and responsive, the answer may be 'yes'. It is that possibility which in this chapter I want to explore.

We should note, however, that the passing of the older concept is not without controversy. The separable, transcendent

---

[2] *Honest to God*, London, 1963, pp. 29–63. He refers to the opening section of Tillich's *Systematic Theology*, Vol. II, Chicago, 1957 pp. 5–12, but the fuller statements are in Vol. I, (Chicago, 1951) pp. 163 ff.

'Wholly Other' concept of God has dominated men's minds for so long, particularly in Western civilisation, that in order to break free from it some theologians, notably Tillich, have not at times shrunk from describing themselves as 'atheistic'. Others again have capitalised on the way in which this type of God-concept has revealed its irrelevance to the present generation by borrowing from Nietzsche the phrase 'the death of God'. As I understand him, William Hamilton wants among other things to draw out the implications of man's 'coming of age', a phrase he has taken from Bonhoeffer, though, indeed, it had already been popularised by Robinson.[3] 'To say that man has "come of age" does not mean that man can solve all his problems, but it does mean that he no longer expects God to intervene miraculously to deliver him from difficult situations. Instead he looks upon the various questions and problems of life as his own task and responsibility. More specifically, he views his needs and problems as matters calling not for religious or devotional acts but for the intelligent application of human effort. For Hamilton this means that God has disappeared as a "need-fulfiller" and a "problem-solver".'[4] Such a theology (or atheism) is desirable in the sense that it reflects the facts of modern life. We no longer pray for rain or deliverance from the plague; we build dams and practise hygiene. For those whose thinking is still formulated in biblical metaphors it may be difficult, indeed distressing, to have to accommodate the thought that the metaphor of 'the good Shepherd' (or even of 'Our Father who is Heaven' as popularly conceived) might be blasphemous, but just as God is not the 'God-of-the-gap' in

---

[3] *Op. cit.* pp. 36–39.
[4] *The Death of God Controversy*, Thomas W. Ogletree, Nashville, 1966, p. 33. Cf. also the article 'The Death of God' by Professor Alastair McKinnon, Associate Professor of Philosophy at McGill, in *The Christian Outlook*, April, 1966, pp. 3–7, and especially the paper by Wilfred Cantwell Smith 'The Death of God?' in *Questions of Religious Truth*, New York, 1967, pp. 13–36.

scientific thought, so too he cannot be the 'God-of-salvation' in social and personal existence.

In what way, then, can we speak of God, if at all? I come back to the point that the question we are interested in is the existential question—'Am I alone?'. This, and the primary question 'Who am I?', are existential questions: the answer to them conditions my existence. All other questions are intellectual and we will come to them, or at least some of them, in time. But for the present we still have the second question of existence to answer: 'Am I alone?'.

As we have seen, this is another way of asking, is my sense of being a person meaningful? I am a physical organism, the brain of which has produced patterns of cortical activity which have given me the notion of myself, and thereby paradoxically freed me from the tyranny of the cortex. Is this something truly significant, the most significant thing about me, and about the process of evolution which led up to it, and about the universe, which is not merely the setting for, but the very stuff of, that process; or is it just a conjuring trick, clever but meaningless? If it is the former, then the fact that I am a person will not be an anomaly with regard to the rest of the system, an accidental evolutionary bi-product of no more significance than the hooked fifth metatarsus in reptiles or Darwin's lobe in the human ear, but it will have shown itself to be part of, indeed as far as I can judge, the goal of the cosmic process on this planet. What that same process is attempting elsewhere in this vast universe I do not know, and at present have small means of ever finding out, though the possibility of beginning that discovery is now for the first time in human history becoming conceivable.[5] But as far as this planet is concerned, either

---

[5] The likelihood that life is present on this planet only is so small that we can confidently expect to discover other life-systems on other planets in our galaxy. Cf. *We are Not Alone; The Search for Intelligent Life on Other Worlds*, Walter Sullivan, New York, 1964. Cf. also the ending of Alice Meynell's perceptive little poem, 'Christ in the Universe':

the life-process by intention and design achieved the emergence of personality as the goal of its operation, or I am the odd-man-out of existence, a creature adapted for swimming in a world that has no water, a sexual nature in a world without sex, a creative musician in a world where there are no tones.

I find that it is literally impossible for me to believe this latter alternative. This is an existential question and to exist, and to continue existing, I have to answer this second existential question as positively as I did the first. To 'believe' is itself a highly personal activity and on this question I cannot 'believe' the negative any more than a man can throw himself whole-heartedly into a lack of enthusiasm. I can 'accept' the negative, I can 'behave' the negative, but I cannot 'believe' it. To believe that my personhood is to be taken seriously calls on me to be more of a person; to accept the opposite calls for a diminishing personal effort. Truth, goodness, beauty, love become, in the latter instance, mere whims and fancies. Life itself becomes a lesser thing. To answer the second existential question negatively is, therefore, as with the first, to deny my own vitality and to begin to destroy myself. Ecclesiastes is a lesser man than Job. There is the smell of death about Lucian, Voltaire, Sartre, but there is the pulse of life, my life, in Plato, Spinoza, Chardin.

I can, of course, accept the negative. I can 'behave' my own negation. I can decide that the universe is indifferent to me. But from that moment, I have precluded myself from a poten-tial which could otherwise have been mine. In this universe, one chooses life, or one has thereby chosen death. By not choosing

But in the eternities
Doubtless we shall compare together, hear
A million alien gospels, in what guise
He trod the Pleiades, the Lyre, the Bear.
Oh be prepared, my soul,
To read the inconceivable, to scan
The infinite forms of God those stars unroll,
When, in our turn, we show to them a Man.

to believe in the ultimate worth of my personhood, I would shut myself off from further personal development. I would have chosen death. To exist, to choose life, and to have it ever more abundantly, I have to believe that my personality is meaningful, is, indeed, the most meaningful fact in the whole story of terrestrial evolution.

Given that analysis of my situation I have no choice. It is the nature of life to choose existence rather than non-existence. I have seen in the sterile Dead Sea desert, one single plant persisting to live. I have seen where the lichen struggles to climb the Rocky Mountains to the very limit of the line of perpetual snow; I am told that in the darkest ocean depths, life adapts to enormous pressures in order to continue to exist. I can be no exception. If to believe is to choose life, then I must believe. This is involved in my initial belief-affirmation, and thereafter I have to live in that faith.[6]

But to make that affirmation of faith in my own personhood, is to imply something about the life-process in the universe itself. It means that the quality of personhood is inherent in the life process itself. Biologically I am the aggregate of a large number of colonies of individually-programmed cells co-ordinated into an organism which is my body, the physical basis of my personality. So, too, the universe, as far as I understand it, is the aggregate of vast numbers of colonies bound in one over-all system, in which even Earth's planetal heat-exchange packet is but one unit. That universe I can reasonably conceive to be integrated by its life as my total organism is integrated by mine. Traditionally we have called that integration 'God'. Then life is God and God is life. God is not other than the universe; he is the universe. God is not other than life; he is life. God is the universe, life, in its personal aspect. He is the personal response of the universe to my personal existence. He transcends the universe as mind transcends the

[6] See above, Chapter I, p. 22 and the end of Chapter II, p. 51.

59

body. He transcends all my thinking of him, for I am very ignorant. But he is not other than the life around me. He is that life. And the quality of personhood can not be alien to him, for it is life which has constituted personhood as the goal and crown of evolution in the terrestrial ecology.

This is not to say that God is a person, for this would be too restricting, but it is to say that life, God, holds within itself the quality of being personal. Thus I shall be doing less violence to the English language to continue to use the pronouns 'he, him' rather than 'it'. On the other hand, I cannot say 'there is a god', for that is an inventory-type, categorising statement, but I do say 'God is', for he is a quality which pervades all existence. After the parallel of the famous description of electricity—'electricity is not a thing but the way things behave'—God is not a person but is the personal way the universe responds. God is not the universe, but the way I know it.[7] He is the fifth dimension of reality.[8]

The hall-mark of personality is, as we have said, the capacity to respond to another person and to need that response in return. When I acknowledge my own personhood, I *ipso facto*

[7] This is a dangerous sentence for it appears to reduce God to being one attribute of the universe—a procedure which certainly would satisfy neither Anselm's *aliquid quo nihil majus cogitari potest*, nor the 'religious instincts' of more average minds. But just as Jones is not to be identified with his body, and yet Jones' personhood is the way in which I know the totality of Jones, so the physical universe is not God, but God is the personal mode of my knowing and being known by the universe, by life, by the totality of reality, call it what you will. God is for us the experience of being met as a person by life.

[8] John Baillie in *Our Knowledge of God*, London, 1939, asks us to start from 'the indubitable fact' of God, and says that all men believe in God in their hearts and only doubt him with 'the top of their minds' (pp. 60–61). I believe I am saying very much the same thing when I say that all men know life, but only some are conscious of that personal quality therein, which I have called 'the fifth dimension', and which traditionally is called 'God'. Cf. 'The believer finds in the most familiar experiences of life a meaning and a presence which the unbeliever does not find in them; and it is on this basis alone that he is able to proceed to those further experiences which the unbeliever cannot have at all.' *Op. cit.* p. 53.

look for that response to come from the life-process which engendered me. It is not enough that I receive that assurance of personhood from my fellows; I must receive it from the universe itself. And I believe I do so receive it. This is a further affirmation of belief. When I look down on the green hills and domestic valleys of a landscape in the Cotswolds or on the pine-clad shores of the mountain-ringed lakes of the Laurentians and am awed by the sense of beauty which possesses me; when an ordered sequence of sounds built up into the majesty of Beethoven's Fifth moves me profoundly to tears; or when I leave a theatre wholly challenged by the revelation of the greatness of goodness in the human soul, as I was when I emerged on a New York street from a performance of *A Man for All Seasons;* then I am aware that there is in the very stuff of the universe that which calls to me to be more of a person than I am, in order to comprehend it and experience it more fully. To experience rationality in the nature of things, in, for example, the concept of the periodic table of chemical elements, or in the knowledge that the same forces which hold the solar system together also operate within the atom, and to reflect that I as a rational being can apprehend that fact and be filled with wonder, again assures me that my personal quality of life is catered for in the very nature of the universe. I as a person am thereby profoundly reassured, just as the adolescent whom we mentioned earlier is reassured when he finds that his elders and betters do take him seriously and do treat him as an adult. When we speak of God, therefore, we are referring to that in the universe which meets us at the personal level. If we are awakened to be aware of it, this experience greets us twenty times a day, in the ordinary incidents of daily living, and this experience is God.

I have therefore answered my second existential question 'Am I alone?' by affirming that I am not alone, that there is Someone with me, and that it is his response to my personhood which confirms my own integrity. Unless God be God, I cannot be I. But I am, and God is. I begin then to know something of the possibilities in St. Augustine's *quia fecisti nos ad te et inquietum est cor nostrum donec requiescat in te*—'thou didst make us oriented towards thee, and our hearts are unquiet until they rest in thee'.[9]

[9] *Confessions*, I, i.

Chapter Four

AN UNDERSTANDING OF THE
NATURAL SCIENCES

THERE is in one of Job's outbursts a wording of a universal longing, so apt and so expressive that men have borrowed it constantly in every generation since the poem first appeared. Referring to God, he cries: 'Oh that I knew where I might find him!'[1] J. S. Whale cleverly began his chapter on God in his Cambridge lectures on the Christian Religion by saying: 'But is there a God? Apparently not. God is not apparent to our senses'.[2]

It is a fact that if God is, he is elusive. Many earnest and intelligent seekers have sought long and with great sincerity and have ended their search unconvinced that they have found anything. This confronts us with a serious problem. If God is the personal response of life to the personhood of man, how comes it that so many men and women are oblivious of it, indeed apparently incapable of sensing it? We can whittle the magnitude of the problem down by saying that many disqualify themselves by turning all their attention elsewhere, that is, to

[1] Job 23:3. The patriarch was in fact seeking for God in order to compel justice from him, but the saying (as so often with much-used quotations) is generally divorced from its context to express the universal longing for an answer to man's deepest questions.

[2] J. S. Whale, *Christian Doctrine*, Cambridge, 1942.

the satisfactions afforded by work or sex or wealth or fame or power; and that others are prevented from any such discovery by the sheer rigidity of the ideas of God they bring to the search[3] (when they do not find precisely what they were looking for, they are convinced they have found nothing); and that other intelligent and decent men have turned away in disgust from religion because its devotees have often behaved stupidly and cruelly and immorally; but even so the problem remains. The author of Second Esdras recognised it in the first century of our era and found no answer other than to state the facts as he saw them: 'The Most High made this world for the sake of many, but the world to come for the sake of few ... Just as when you ask the earth, it will tell you that it provides very much clay from which earthenware is made and only a little dust from which gold comes; so is the course of the present world. Many have been created, but few shall be saved.'[4] The writer was manifestly not happy with the facts, but he had to accept them. We too have to recognise that if the goal of the cosmic process on this planet is the emergence of personality in man, and if the response of the personal in man to the personal in the universe is the fulfilment of his being, then it is comparatively few who are sensitive to these things. And anyone

[3] This is why I think it was important to start this enquiry from an anthropological base and with the blank page of humanism, rather than with preconceived theistic concepts, particularly those of the so-called 'revealed theology'. It is also why I have found little of significance for my personal enquiry in the logomachies of the linguistic analytical school of philosophy. Whether one can make a meaningful statement about God surely depends on the connotation placed by the speaker on the word 'God': 'Yahweh of hosts is most holy' signified a very great deal to Isaiah of Jerusalem because of the concept he had of Yahweh rather than because he was aware of 'restrictive theories about the way in which words and, derivatively, statements or utterances can function.' Cf. the paper from which this phrase is taken 'Religious Language and the Assumptions of Belief', Alastair McKinnon, *The Christian Scholar*, XLIX, 1, Spring, 1966, pp. 50–59, and also Donald Evans *The Logic of Self-Involvement*, London, 1963. Dr Evans, a former colleague, is now Associate Professor of Philosophy in the University of Toronto.

[4] 2 Esdras 8:2–3.

working in a university has to add that it is often the more intelligent, the more responsible, the more mature, the more likeable people, who lack religious interests.[5] I believe this to be the tragedy of our times, and can only hope that it is a situation (almost I had said a 'fashion') which will pass. This is no cry for religious orthodoxy on the campus, but it is a plea for a return to ultimate concern by the more intelligent elements in modern society.

But if God is, then I at least must seek him and seek to know more and more about him. This is the question to which I would have thought no intelligent man could be indifferent, but I at least must address myself to it: how can I find out about God? 'Oh that I knew where I might find him!'

If God is 'the fifth dimension of reality' then the obvious place to begin is with the natural order. As he explores the human situation, man necessarily investigates both his environment and himself. The former gives rise to the natural, that is the physical and biological, sciences and the latter to the social sciences and the humanities. These categories, of course, intermingle very considerably but they serve as the broad distinctions. The task of the natural sciences is easier, and very much more quickly-rewarding than that of the social sciences and the humanities, and thus it is not surprising that the natural sciences have made the greater progress and have produced the more impressive results. Man's scientific discoveries over the last one hundred and fifty years constitute a wholly new and determinative phenomenon in the history of this planet, and those of the last fifteen years are overwhelming in their range and their complexity. It is doubtful even now whether the computer, and the new discipline of cybernetics as applied to information-retrieval, will be able to prevent the whole process

---

[5] I suspect that anyone working in any large corporation—business, the civil service, the Army, for example—would often be compelled to make the same judgement.

from clogging down simply by reason of its own uncontrolled proliferation. Robert Sinsheimer began an address given to the Caltech Seventy-fifth Anniversary Conference with a striking illustration, reminding us how recently all this new knowledge has been gained: '... on the towering cliffs of gorges in Utah and Arizona one can read hundreds of millions of years of earth's history. On that immense scale a foot represents the passage of perhaps a hundred thousand years; all of man's recorded history took place as an inch was deposited; all of organised science, a millimeter; all we know of genetics, a few tens of microns.'[6] Man's scientific knowledge is new, and it is relatively disorganised, undigested and incoherent, but it is already re-writing his destiny and it is increasing at an incredible pace. To ignore it in any account of ultimate issues would be folly indeed. At a recent theological conference, at the conclusion of a paper on the Doctrine of God, a paper which discussed very learnedly the biblical and historical-theological data, one critic remarked that this must be the only subject of intelligent discussion where a scholar could responsibly assume that what is to be said today is unchanged from what might have been said one hundred years ago. The critic then challenged that assumption and surely was right to do so. If God is the living God, then we should know more of him than we did a century ago; if he is the personal response of the universe to my personhood, then all the new knowledge of that universe has a very great deal to say to me about him.

It is nevertheless a mistake to look into the natural sciences for detail to be used to establish the classical teleological argument concerning purposeful design in nature. It is tempting to consider, for example, the fact that water becomes more dense as it loses heat until it reaches $4°C$ but thereafter as it

---

[6] The address was significantly entitled 'The End of the Beginning'; cf. *The Bulletin of the California Institute of Technology*, Vol. 76, No. 1, March 1967. Robert Sinsheimer is Professor of Biophysics at the Institute.

becomes colder it reverses the tendency and becomes less dense. The argument thereafter asserts that consequently ice forms first on the top, not at the bottom, of lakes and rivers and the sea, and that but for this simple little characteristic of water, fish would be frozen up out of water in northern latitudes, and northern lake and sea life as we know it would have been quite impossible. This is then put forward as a clear instance of the environment being adapted to the needs of life, rather than the usual adaptation of life to the environment. The catch is, of course, that if lakes had frozen from the bottom up fish and other water creatures would have adapted to that environment, just as they have to the present situation, by contriving to hibernate frozen solid deep in the ice each winter, or by migrating as winter approached, as do in fact many birds (and also at least some fish), or by becoming seasonal amphibia, or by choosing some other way of surmounting the environmental difficulty. To find teleogy in this or that detail of the natural order is thus a very doubtful procedure.[7] Nevil Shute has a story (which proved in its major theme to be grimly prophetic) of an intellectual genius in the field of nuclear physics, who during the day calculated mathematically an experimentally undemonstrated fatigue factor in metals which could cause a plane to crash, but who in the evening calculated with equal seriousness the time of the Second Coming of Jesus from the proportions of the Great Pyramid, and who swallowed wholesale the linguistic crudities and historical impossibilities of the British Israel theory. The novel is a telling and by no means forced illustration of the way in which genius in natural science can be accompanied by near mental deficiency in religion. Isaac Newton followed the immortal *Principia* with a study of

[7] My colleague Professor Dunbar informs me that the fact that ice forms first at the surface of rivers and lakes has in any case little to do with water density, but rather with air temperatures. The sea also freezes first at the surface and does not have this density-characteristic, since its water is salt.

Daniel and The Revelation which is irrelevant nonsense because he was not in a position to grasp the nature of apocalyptic writings.[8] The tragedy is that with the best of motives he deliberately turned from the study of science to devote himself to this kind of prognostication. The practice therefore of taking this or that item of scientific knowledge, and finding in it, even on the authority of the most eminent scientist in that particular field, a confirmation of religious theories arrived at on other grounds, is quite unsound. We can too easily reduce the physical order of the universe to a source of allegory, and all an allegory ever does is to illustrate the fertility of invention of the allegorist—it reveals nothing whatsoever about the material allegorised.

In contrast to this wrong and dangerous method of approach, we ought, I suggest, to look at the natural sciences as a totality and ask whether as a whole they have anything to tell us about God. Again let me recall that by 'God' I do not mean a Being separate from and other than the universe, but rather the personal responsiveness of the universe to my sense of person-hood. In looking at the sciences as a whole I am in fact asking what things they have to tell me about their subject-matter which I have to accept and to build into my concept of God. For their subject-matter and my concern are one. Science is in the truest sense of the words 'practical theology'. W. F. Moulton, Headmaster of the Leys School and a truly great biblical scholar, is said to have made sure that the biology lesson followed upon the scripture lesson, so that he could dismiss the boys with the remark 'Now go and learn about God from another point of view'. When we think science, we think God.

As I take a layman's interest in the vast scope of science, and as I listen to my colleagues in the different sciences talk about

[8] Isaac Newton, *Observations upon the Prophecies of Daniel and the Apocalypse of St John*, London, 1733.

their work and the things that excite them, I am greatly impressed by three things—the unity of their universe, their complete acceptance of the idea of evolution, and their readiness to explore the concept of ecology. It is on these ideas that I want to comment.

I referred earlier to man's new knowledge as being still inchoate and disorganised. In one sense this is true, and it is said that all the great advances of our time have been due to one individual, not necessarily that much more intelligent than others, having the good fortune to realise the relevance of two or three seemingly unrelated lines of endeavour. It is largely this recognition which has given rise to the present boom in interdisciplinary studies. Those of us who can recall the jigsaw puzzle of our youth can recognise the situation readily enough. It is not merely that the key to a problem being worked at in Cambridge, Mass. may well have been forged already in Cambridge, England,—or in Leningrad or Vienna or Tokyo—but also that the work in genetics may take a leap forward because someone recognises the relevance of a new concept in molecular chemistry being explored on the other side of the campus, or of a new discovery relating to immunology in the university hospital. The disciplinary and mental distances are often more difficult to leap than the geographical. Nevertheless, for the scientist, it is an unchallenged premise that truth is one and reason is one. The methodology of thought which is effective in physics and mathematics will also be effective in zoology and botany. Moreover, that methodology will be as apparent and as convincing to a student newly arrived from the University of Katmandu as it is to the product of Oxford or Harvard. There are no 'western' ways of thought in mathematics, no Indian physics, no Muslim geology. Further—and very much further—what is true on earth and in our solar system is also true in the great galaxies that lie far out beyond our own. Astronomy and astrophysics depend wholly on that assumption. For science the universe is indissolubly one.

Then God is one. E. S. Waterhouse used to remark to his students that philosophically there was no compelling argument in favour of monotheism in competition with dualism or polytheism. But science has affirmed that this environment of the human situation is a universe not a multiverse, and if the universe is one then God who is the personal of the universe is One and as such is known, recognised and responded to by the reason which is in man. We are back again at perhaps the most attractive and compelling of all the great ideas of classical Greek philosophy—the Logos doctrine of reason in man and Reason in the universe and the correspondence of the one to the other.[9] God, we may affirm, is One and he is reasonable. We were not, then, very far off course in our first chapter when we said that reason is man's surest, indeed only, guide. Man is reasonable because Nature is reasonable and Nature is reasonable because God is reasonable. I may be here arguing in a circle but it is a circle out of which I by my very nature cannot break. The alternative is chaos, mental, spiritual, scientific. The world's first recorded thinkers, the men of ancient Babylon typified the act of creation as the reduction of chaos to order, that is, to Reason, and that is something on which I cannot go back.[10] The natural sciences thus confirm me in my expectations of the unity and reasonableness of God, and I am thereby

[9] As I write these words, I am conscious of an affinity of spirit not only with the Stoics and Marcus Aurelius, and even Seneca (despite all their unprepossessing characteristics) but also with Confucius and Menucius and especially to Lao-tze, the exponent of *Tao*. The religious enquiry of mankind is not disparate at depth. Cf. R. L. Slater, *World Religions and World Community*, New York and London, 1963. Dr Slater, formerly my colleague as Professor of Systematic Theology at McGill, was later Director of the Center for the Study of World Religions at Harvard University.

[10] Cf. the *'enuma 'elish*, J. B. Pritchard, *Ancient Near Eastern Texts*, Princeton, second edition 1955, p. 60, and the Hebrew derivative, Genesis 1, and especially Genesis 1:2 'and the earth was *thohu wabhohu*' i.e. chaotic.

reassured in the depths of my being. In the language of religion, it is a great 'comfort' to me.[11]

The theory of evolution was not invented by Charles Darwin but it was very largely substantiated by him. He and Wallace hit independently on the idea of natural selection but it was Darwin who demonstrated and established the phenomenon with a truly impressive wealth of data. In the intervening century the evidence has accumulated to the point where it has become overwhelming. All life on this planet, we may confidently affirm, has a common ancestor. The unity of the ecological system and the uniformity of structure inherent in all living matter tend to suggest that however life arose out of matter it did so on this planet historically once and once only. This would suggest that even when the physical conditions are right for the emergence of life, the actual event is exceedingly rare. Incidentally, this consideration is perhaps not sufficiently taken into account by those who speculate on the possibility of life elsewhere in the universe. It by no means follows that because the conditions for life exist, therefore life will exist. We might find—and have thereon to ponder deeply—that 'life' is an exclusively terrestrial phenomenon. On the other hand, the number of planets capable of producing life is so huge that it seems incredible that what has happened here has not also happened many, many times elsewhere. We shall just have to wait and see.[12]

Nevertheless we have no reason to doubt that the emergence of life on this planet, rare event as it was, was even so a normative and regular part of the planetary process. Indeed the whole of biological evolution is but the extrapolation of a process of development which had been in process for thou-

[11] In the sense that the Holy Spirit is 'the Comforter', i.e. the one who reassures, strengthens, makes firm. The ordered reasonableness of the natural order as deriving from the ordered reasonableness of God is also the theme of the appendix to the Flood myth, Genesis 8: 20–22.

[12] Cf. note 5, Chapter III.

sands of millions of years (if the concept 'years' has any significance here) previously. 'In the beginning', of our solar system
there was probably a cloud of thinly-diffused gas, possibly of
hydrogen. This was acted upon by forces in the vastness of
space in ways we do not yet understand, so that it densified
and increased in temperature until it was the swirling, flaming,
exploding mass which we call the sun. As the temperature and
pressures built up, the 'complexification' of matter (to use
Teilhard de Chardin's word) continued. Atoms were split,
nuclei and electrons re-arranged themselves into differing
patterns to produce new elements, haphazardly no doubt in
time but in an orderly progression as regards structure.[13]
Parts of the flaming mass were thrown off into space but were
unable to escape the magnetic pull of the mother who had given
them birth and they went into orbit around her and became the
planets. On these planets, the atoms of the elements combined
to form molecules of complex substances and the molecules
built up into chains, and from the simple building blocks of
the elements, intricate and complicated structures of matter
began to take shape—forming the earth and sea and atmosphere.
Eventually, on our planet, at least, there appeared the earlier
forms of self-producing matter, what we call 'life'. At that time,
earth almost certainly had an oxygen-free atmosphere. A. I.
Oparin suggested it was predominantly a water-methane
atmosphere and J. B. S. Haldane that it was predominantly a
carbon-dioxide atmosphere. The suggestions follow that either
the lighter hydrogen molecules were torn from the water in the
atmosphere out into space again, or that the bombardment of
the atmosphere by solar rays produced photosynthesis of
carbon compounds by primitive plants; either way oxygen was

[13] Thus it was that Mendeléyev's 'Periodic System of the Elements' could
be formulated. From the relationships of known elements the existence of
unknown elements could be predicted. The latter have now been discovered
and the list is continuous from 1 to 103. New elements, beyond 103, may be
expected to result from nuclear reactions.

released into the atmosphere. This was indeed a major event, the so-called 'oxygen revolution'. The higher forms of life as we know it, then became possible, and the story of biological evolution began to unfold. Possibly the beginnings were in the oxygenated tidal waters of the sea. Then slowly some forms of life became amphibious, and finally terrestrial. We may well be wrong on the detail, but we have reason to believe that this over-all picture corresponds fairly closely to the facts.

The significant recognition of our own generation is that this process of evolution is as inherent in non-living matter as it is in living matter. This planet and presumably the universe at large is one vast evolving system. Indeed it is now customary to distinguish three major phases in evolution—the pre-biological, physical stage; the biological stage, when natural selection alone determined the process; and the post-biological, that is, the stage when man's intelligence emerged and began to direct first his own evolution and now increasingly that of his fellow creatures and indeed of his planet. 'Evolution in the most general terms is a natural process of irreversible change, which generates novelty, variety and increase of organisation: and all reality can be regarded in one aspect as evolution. Biological evolution is only one sector or phase of this total process. There is also the inorganic or cosmic sector and the psychosocial or human sector. The phases succeed each other in time, the later being based on and evolving out of the earlier. The inorganic phase is pre-biological, the human is post-biological. Each sector or phase has its own characteristic method of operation, proceeds at its own tempo, possesses its own possibilities and limitations, and produces its own characteristic results. . . .' So wrote Julian Huxley in a discussion of evolution since the time of Darwin, and in a salute to the great scientist he adds: 'This centennial celebration is one of the first occasions on which it has been frankly faced that all aspects of reality are subject to evolution, from atoms and stars to fish

73

and flowers, from fish and flowers to human societies and values—indeed that all reality is a single process of evolution. And ours is the first period in which we have acquired sufficient knowledge to begin to see the outline of this vast process as a whole.' Elsewhere he writes: 'Evolution—or to spell it out, the idea of the evolutionary process—is the most powerful and the most comprehensive idea that has ever arisen on earth.'[14] I have to agree with Huxley—evolution is the most comprehensive idea that has ever arisen on earth, and I am forced to conclude that there is not room in one and the same universe for separate ideas of God and evolution, any more than there is room for separate concepts of God and life. When I speak of the one, I speak of the other, and I am reminded of Studdert-Kennedy's line 'Some call it Evolution, and others call it God'. Change, growth, and development are then inherent in the nature of God. The Hebrews saw clearly when they called Yahweh 'the Living God'.

Closely associated with the idea of evolution is the third of these major concepts of contemporary science, that of ecology and the ecosystem. The physical elements, as determined by the geomorphological and climatic conditions, provide the environment for, and play a large part in determining the characteristics of, a nexus of relationships of flora and fauna, in which everybody lives by taking in everybody's washing and everybody can survive only by minding everybody else's business. Grasses and plants depend on insects and birds for pollination and seed distribution, herbivores crop the vegetation, carnivores prey on one another. The remarkable thing about an ecosystem is its delicacy of balance, and its inbuilt system of checks and controls. If one species becomes too abundant, it runs into a shortage of food supply and at the same time, by having made existence easier for its predators, it increases the number of its natural enemies and the balance begins to be restored. My

[14] *Essays of a Humanist*, London and Toronto, 1964, pp. 29, 74, 125.

colleague Professor Maxwell Dunbar has pointed out that violent oscillations of the elements constituting an ecosystem is in fact a sign of immaturity—the area is thereby shown to be one which life has colonised more recently than it did those areas where the system is more stable, and he points to the relative regularity of ecosystems in the tropics as compared with the relative instability of those in the subarctic. He also draws attention to the operation of the factor of natural selection in the collapse of unstable ecosystems and their replacement by systems more able to achieve stability of operation. The evolutionary process is clearly at work on this larger, ecological scale as well as within the development of a particular species.[15]

We have to recognise, however, that the identification of an ecosystem is the act of the ecologist. It is he who says, let us take this area, this particular segment of terrestrial functioning and let us consider it as a unit. Actually, of course, it is part of the larger system which is our whole planet. Our earth with its atmosphere is one total heat-exchange unit, receiving energy from the sun, using it and discharging it again into space—and very significantly suffering in the process from an imbalance of operation, in a manner reminiscent of the 'balance of payments' problems of national economies. The Earth seems steadily to be paying out more than it is taking in, and so by the notorious Second Law of Thermodynamics we are inevitably one day going to run out of energy and the vast ecosystem we call Earth is going to collapse in a universal death. But this fate waits not only the planet Earth but also the whole solar system of which it is but one small part. Whether this is also to be the eventual fate of the universe at large is one of the unanswered questions of our time.

Most people, knowing that that settlement day is many

---

[15] 'The Evolution of Stability in Marine Environments; Natural Selection at the Level of the Ecosystem' in *The American Naturalist*, March–April, 1960, XCIV, No. 875, pp. 129–136.

millions of years in the future, are prepared to dismiss the problem cheerfully from their minds, but the philosophical and religious implications remain. If the evolutionary process is going forward, where is it going to, does it have a goal, will it end in a bang or, as T. S. Eliot feared, only in a whimper? One of the noticeable characteristics of biological writing is that it strenuously insists that natural selection is uncontrolled and adventitious. The characteristic of chance is central to the very concept. This is agreed on all sides. Even so, one is surprised to read in biological papers sentence after sentence which imply that adaptations were designed to meet various conditions and eventualities and that the whole process is intelligently directed. I quote but one instance out of very many, but this one is particularly noticeable because it comes from a paper discussing the very subject and assuming that the customary rejection of intelligent direction of evolution is unchallengeably correct: 'The entities and physical systems that exist at any period have been selected by nature because of their "fitness" to endure'. This, my colleagues in the biological sciences tell me, somewhat ruefully, is a habit of mind into which they are constantly prone to fall. They realise its inconsistency, they try to avoid it, but it is an error which they find themselves making involuntarily, simply because it is quicker and easier to think and talk that way rather than to stop each time and use the circuitous language of chance and natural selection.

This seems to me, however, to be more significant than simply an unfortunate and recurrent lapse of speech, and I gather that it is beginning to appear significant to at least some of the biologists. It would seem that just as animism is anathema to the behaviourist psychologist, and yet, as we saw, some accommodation with the idea is necessary if man is to remain man, so teleology is of the devil in the eyes of all biologists, and yet the notion of goals and ends in the struggle for existence is so undeniable, that some place for a modified

76

form of teleology may have to be found in biological thinking. I am reminded of Mark Tapley, who in *Martin Chuzzlewit* set out to be a philosopher but try as he would 'cheerfulness would keep breaking in'. Similarly the biologists (so it seems to me) try very hard to work with evolution and ecology as purely fortuitous processes but the sense that in their general drift they are directed towards an end or goal is too strong to be denied. Grace A. de Laguna discusses the point in the very interesting paper, quoted from above, in which she points out that Colin S. Pittendrigh has proposed the term 'teleonomy' to take the place of the rejected 'teleology'.[16] What biologists, she writes, 'reject as "teleology" is the doctrine that the results of evolutionary process, the production of the living cell, and later of intelligent man—are *ends*, or goals, to which these processes have been directed by some external or internal controlling agency'. But she points out that these same biologists find it impossible to deny that at every stage of evolution there is in fact an end-directedness. At the pre-biological, chemical stage of evolution the end is increasing complexity of structure: 'There is, of course, no such body of direct evidence for the evolutionary origin of life as is available for the fact of bio-logical evolution. We are, however, committed to the accept-ance of an inorganic evolution as the only reasonable hypo-thesis, although science is unable to trace the steps by which the earliest primitive organisms were evolved from non-living matter and energy. There is evidence that earlier terrestrial conditions of atmosphere and oceans were favourable to the slow accumulation of organic materials. It is to be supposed that many complex chemical substances were spontaneously formed, many of them to disintegrate under changing condi-tions. The course of evolution in all its stages is marked by the

[16] 'The Rôle of Teleonomy in Evolution', *The Philosophy of Science*, Vol. 29 No. 2, April 1962, pp. 117–131. Cf. Colin S. Pittendrigh, 'Adaptation, Natural Selection and Behaviour' in *Behaviour and Evolution*, ed. Anne Roe and George Gaylord Simpson, Newhaven, 1958, p. 394f.

production of structures of increasing complexity.' At the biological stage of evolution, she continues, the ends are survival and reproduction, but not mere replication but also the production of genetic variations which will allow new species to emerge, to stabilise their forms and become the next link in the chain of increasing complexity of structure and adaptation. In the post-biological, the cultural stage of evolution, the end-directedness becomes clearly apparent as man, more and more consciously, takes control of all life and modifies it to his purposes. We may illustrate this by recalling that man ruthlessly wipes out the innumerable buffalo herds of North America, suppresses the mosquito in the malarial swamps of Panama, and robs small-pox of its power to ravage whole human populations, while at the same time breeding new herds of cattle in Great Britain, developing new types of wheat for the Prairies, and cultivating new strains of bacteria for use in his hospitals and laboratories. It becomes increasingly difficult to deny that there is in all this grand sweep of evolution an end-directedness: increasing complexity, survival, reproduction, development, intelligence. Hence Pittendrigh's invention of the term 'teleonomy', which recognises the directedness towards a 'telos' or end, but makes no comment on who or what is doing the directing.[17] As Professor de Laguna puts it in the

[17] Pittendrigh writes 'adaptation as a genuine scientific problem was obscured up to 1859 by its association with Aristotelian teleology; and since 1859 it has had a hard time shedding a guilt acquired by that former association . . . Organisation is universally recognised to be characteristic of life as evidenced by the general use of "organism" for a living system. . . . Organisation is always relative, and relative to an end; it differs from mere order in this respect. . . . The importance of this point for the student of living systems is that he cannot lightly assert they are organised without being prepared to face the question: "with respect to what are they organised?" There simply is no meaning to the word organisation that will safeguard him against this question which so many biologists evidently sought to avoid. And there is little excuse for avoiding the simpler wording: "To what end is the living system organised?" Thus to say that living things are organised is to say that they are adapted. It is only the vagary of usage that has so far protected "organisation" from the fatal connotation of "teleology".

abstract of her paper, the biologists who accept the term do so 'only as descriptive and neglecting its significance for theory'. This seems to me permissible. At the level of the single instance, the element of chance operates as far as any observer can determine, quite freely. But, as the mathematical science of statistics shows, the individual can be subject to chance, while the group or class is subject to discernible laws. Insurance life-expectancy tables are a case in point. In evolution, at the individual level, the mechanism is chance, but taking the process as a whole there is a steady drift towards increased complexity, survival and variant reproduction. To describe the drift by the term 'teleonomy' is then reasonable—it indicates that the process is operating under the 'law' of end-directedness without implying 'whose' law it is, and this, I can recognise, gives the biologist the freedom he needs. He has to have the liberty to do his own tasks of experimentation and discovery; he must be free to observe, to deduce, to hypothesise. He must therefore be allowed to work at the isolated problem with the notion of undirected evolution, and, when he steps back a little and surveys a larger segment of life, with the notion of teleonomy. No scientist can be expected to work properly with God breathing down his neck all the time.[18]

Nevertheless, I suggest that Professor de Laguna and her colleagues cannot get wholly away with this simple 'neglect of

---

Neither term in fact necessarily implies teleology but both do imply teleonomy.' *op. cit.* pp. 392, 394–395. Cf. also the Foreword by Lawrence K. Frank to 'Teleogical Mechanisms', *Annals of the New York Academy of Sciences*, Vol. 50, Art. 4, pp. 187–278 (October 1948).

[18] Cf. J. S. Habgood, 'The Uneasy Truce Between Science and Theology', *Soundings*, ed. A. R. Vidler, Cambridge, 1962, p. 26: 'Likewise scientists, if they care about theology at all, are generally anxious to keep it quite separate from science, because as soon as theological notions are introduced into science research comes to a full stop. Some sort of language about purpose and design, for example, is indispensable to biology; but every biologist knows that if he uses these words too loosely, and especially if he tries to read theological implications into them then he will soon stop asking the sort of question which produces scientific results.'

theory'. It is, of course, another way of saying 'Let's not ask ultimate questions in science'. This again is perfectly legitimate. The natural sciences neither ask nor answer ultimate questions. But no one can be a scientist a hundred per cent of his time; every scientist has from time to time to resume full manhood, and for man standing on a shrinking planet in an expanding universe and trying to understand the human situation, ultimate questions are inescapable.[19]

For myself, aware of myself as the product of evolution and as sustained in a complex ecological system, but even more aware of myself as a person requiring a personal response from life, I cannot 'neglect the theory'. I have to push questions to their ultimate issue, and I cannot believe in the purposelessness of life. I, at least, find myself compelled to believe that there is an intelligible significance in all existence, that evolution in all its phases is the vast outworking of a great design, that I am part of that pattern, and that I shall only be fully satisfied when I have discovered the meaning of the universe and latched the endeavour of my little existence to the significance of the whole. That is what I believe it means in modern terms to be a religious man. Such a man will understand that the biologists will use the term and concept 'teleonomy'— expressing the thought that evolution proceeds towards its *telos* under a *nomos* or law of end-directedness—but the philosopher and the theologian and the religious man will find a deeper meaning in the term 'teleology'—that the end-directedness of evolution is directed towards its *telos* by a *logos* or reason, the personal quality of the universe, God. Evolution and ecology are in this

---

[19] The new feature on the university campus is the increasing attention being paid to 'the philosophy of science'. It remains to be seen whether this new discipline will fare more successfully than 'the philosophy of history' or 'the philosophy of religion'. It may content itself with taking its colouration from current philosophy proper and ask such questions as 'how may scientific hypotheses be properly expressed', or it may go on to recognise the implications of the scientific world-view for man's existential questions and thus revive an interest in the metaphysical in philosophy as a whole.

view intelligently directed by use of the mechanism of adaptation and natural selection towards goals which are only now in
this age of cultural evolution beginning to reveal themselves.
'Ear has not heard, eye has not seen, nor has it entered into the
heart of man, what things God has prepared for them that love
him.'

Some major questions remain—or rather now for the first
time begin to present themselves. The primary question is, 'if
evolution is God at work in the universe, how are we to think
of him?' This question alone[20] is far too great for my answering,
but at least it arouses in me the desire to say two things.

The meaning of human existence is beginning to emerge, I
have suggested, in terms of a relationship of individual personality with a personal response from the universe. The universe is meaningful in personal terms, and each one of us can
be part of that meaningfulness. This is no new thought, but
has indeed been the ground of the religious man's 'love' of
God and his sense of being 'loved' by him. Metaphors, such as

[20] A hardly lesser question is, what in an evolutionary ecological universe
is the nature of love? To some, as to Tennyson, it seemed that if God is
love, as St John affirmed, then God and Nature must be at strife, and that
Nature, red in tooth and claw with ravine, shrieks against any faith in love as
the quality of the universe (*In Memoriam*, LVI, v.). It may be that as we
rethink God, so we must reconceptualise love. Gavin Maxwell in *A Ring of
Bright Water* tells of wading in the sea so packed with herring fry that it was
like wading in silver treacle; they were hemmed into the shores of the little
bay by a swarm of mackerel, but these in their turn, even while they fed on
the herring fry, were being harried by a school of porpoises, and even they
found themselves unable to retreat. 'Beyond them black against the sunset
water, rose the towering sabre fin of a killer whale, his single terrible form
controlling by his mere presence the billions of lives between him and the
shore.' What does that say of God, who is the personal response of that kind
of world to human personality? First—I offer the thoughts tentatively but
with considerable conviction—that we must not look for that personal quality
of response elsewhere than at the personal level of existence, what Teilhard
de Chardin called 'the noosphere', the realm of the mind. To do so would be
truly inappropriate. But secondly that to be fed and in turn to feed is at every
level the true nature of love. At the level of biology this principle gives rise
to a vast ecosystem of eating and being eaten, an unbroken sacrament of
life; at the level of mind it is knowing and being known, as in Psalm 139:
1f. and 1 Corinthians 13:12b.

those of the shepherd and his lamb, of the father and his son, or even of the lover and his loved-one, have traditionally expressed the conviction. I am very aware of the unreal sentimentality of much of this piety. Whatever God is, he is not sentimental, and the metaphor of the shepherd has surely outlived its usefulness. If we can still use the metaphor of father and son, we do not have in mind an adult-child relationship, but rather that of a father and a mature, independent, fully-responsible son. The relationship of God and man is the relationship of adult and adult, and the metaphor of the lover and his beloved, the erotic element being not purged but rather elevated to the mystical, is probably the most expressive in this time when man has 'come of age' before God. For this last is what the term 'cultural evolution' truly implies.

But in a mature relationship there can be, there must be, profound mutual respect and on the part of the beloved an unfathomable awe. I have over many years found great significance in the lines of John Mason:

> *How great a being, Lord, is thine,*
> *Which doth all beings keep!*
> *Thy knowledge is the only line*
> *To sound so vast a deep.*
> *Thou art a sea without a shore,*
> *A sun without a sphere;*
> *Thy time is now and evermore,*
> *Thy place is everywhere.*

My small understanding of the natural sciences deepens in me profoundly that sense of awe. I also ponder the story of St Francis who once, when on a journey, stayed overnight in a monastery. The abbot gave him a bed in his own cell, in order that he might be edified by observing the saint at his devotions. To his host's surprise, Francis said no prayers at all, but flung himself on the pallet and was soon fast asleep. The abbot indignantly said more prayers than usual, and went off to sleep in a glow of self-righteousness. But in the night he awoke and saw Francis, kneeling in a patch of moonlight and looking out of the window into the dark of the night beyond. He was saying one word only, over and over again, 'God . . . God . . . God . . . God . . .'

Chapter Five

AN UNDERSTANDING OF HISTORY

BEGINNING this enquiry, as I believe one must, from the human, existential situation, I have already taken into account some of the considerations which present themselves from those areas of man's understanding which have been organised as 'the social sciences'. I had at the start to take into consideration some of the insights afforded by the studies we know as anthropology and psychology. But anyone who asks 'who am I, where did I come from?' will be particularly concerned with the story of the past experiences of his own species; in other words, he will be deeply interested to know all he can about history and history writing.

For those of us who have been brought up in the christian tradition this concern is particularly important. Christianity has been an historically-minded religion. As Karl Barth points out,[1] the purpose of the inclusion of Pontius Pilate in the Apostles' Creed was to secure an historical reference: the 'Christ-event' took place in history at a particular, identifiable point: *sub Pontio Pilato*, 'when Pontius Pilate was procurator of Judea'. There are very good reasons why Christianity should be thus historically-minded. The basis of all christian thinking is the classical writings of the ancient Hebrew people. There is no parallel in all history to the phenomenon whereby

[1] Cf. Karl Barth, *Credo*, Eng. Trans., London, 1936, pp. 79–82.

84

a great international movement adopted the ancestors, patriotisms, world-view, and aspirations of a single nation and made them so completely its own. But this is what Christianity and consequently the Western European tradition did in the most thorough-going manner: it appropriated the past of the Hebrew nation. A striking illustration of this is that when, by reason of the quite other Greek inheritance in aesthetics, the nineteenth-century agnostic poet and art-critic Matthew Arnold wished to denigrate those who were insensitive to beauty and the artistic skills, it was natural to him to designate them by the name of early Israel's most alien neighbour and indeed enemy, the Philistines. This is in fact a complete reversal of eleventh-century rôles, since the Philistines were a cultured, civilised people far in advance technologically and aesthetically of the still very rustic Hebrews.[2] But emotionally the western tradition identifies with Israel, and thus it is second nature to our poets to dismiss those alien to our own traditions as 'lesser breeds without the Law'.[3] The phenomenon stems from the fact that the Church arose out of Judaism but neither could break, nor desired to break, with its past; rather, the Church insisted that she was the new Israel, indeed the true Israel. Certainly she adopted Israelite religious attitudes, Israelite morality and Israelite literature, together with a ready-made set of Israelite ancestors, Abraham, Isaac, and Jacob, and a ready-made set of Israelite heroes and heroines, from Joseph through to Judith.[4]

[2] The use of the term Philistine in this sense is older than Arnold (the Oxford English Dictionary cites it from 1827) but he was the populariser of the usage ('The people who believe that our greatness and welfare are proved by our being very rich . . . are just the very people whom we call the Philistines'). For the modern estimate of the Philistines see *Biblical Archaeologist* XXII, 1959, pp. 54–56, and pp. 70–102.

[3] Rudyard Kipling, 'Recessional'.

[4] This has led to some very curious 'christian' moral judgements; see my *Patriarchs and Prophets*, Montreal, 1963, especially for the discussion of Samson, pp. 73–82; and also my paper, 'Judgement on Jezebel; or A Woman Wronged'; *Theology Today*, January 1964, pp. 503–517.

Along with these things, and a great deal else, the Church accepted as basic to all her thinking, as it was basic to all Israelite thinking, the Hebrew[5] concept of history. Indeed, the Hebrews invented history.[6] Prior to their time, there were indeed annals and records, for example the Chronicle of Babylon, regularly kept by the priests of that city. But in the eleventh century B.C. the Hebrews passed through a profound experience. At its beginning and through to its third quarter, they were nobodies, seeking to become somebodies. They were looking for a land of their own, on which to settle and become a people, having 'pride of ancestry and hope of posterity.' From the thirteenth through to the eleventh century the dream had flickered, flared up and almost faded altogether as they strove first to infiltrate into Palestine, and then to stay there. But in the last quarter of the eleventh-century, David appeared. In one short life-time, he gave them all that they had dreamed of— a unity of nationhood, a capital city, a national cult, and a hope for future greatness. A Judean priest, of the time, looking back on it all, saw the hand of the Hebrew god Yahweh in these astonishing events, and (once the clue had been given) in the events not merely of David's time, but also in those of a much earlier period. He collected scraps of poetry and aetiologies, myths and legends and remembered events, and he wove them, on the frame-work of a highly-artificial genealogical tree, into one continuous story, the story of Israel's past, showing that from 'the beginning' the creation of Israel as 'the people of God' was the goal to which in all his activity Yahweh had been steadily working. Until now men had thought in terms of

[5] In this context the words 'Hebrew' and 'Israelites' can be used interchangeably; originally 'Hebrew' was an opprobrious term of social status and only used of the group of Hebrews who called themselves 'Israelites' by Gentiles or in a gentile context; the preferred term within the nation was 'Israelite'. 'Jewish' is a post-exilic term applicable to the community when Israel had shrunk practically to the tribe of Judah.

[6] Despite the claims made for Herodotus as 'the Father of History'. See p. 93.

time-cycles, the Annus Magnus, the succession of the Four Ages, Golden, Silver, Bronze, Iron, each inevitably following the other as summer follows on winter and spring, and gives way in turn to autumn and winter once again. The prototype was in fact the agricultural year. But the Hebrew priest (or priests) took that great wheel of time and straightened it out flat, and said 'In the beginning, when the world and time began, God created the heavens and the earth and man ... and all subsequent events led up to this, ourselves as the people of God, (the later term was 'the Kingdom of God') with Zion as his holy place and David as his Messiah'. History, then, is the story of the past told in such a way as to bring out a meaning, and the Hebrews invented it around the tenth century before Christ.[7]

Tied in with this concept were two other ideas. The first was the idea of eschatology, that is, that history is going somewhere and that it has a foreordained goal. This idea first took shape, I have suggested, in the form of 'realised eschatology', that is, 'this present state of affairs is what God has been working up to in his activity in history'. It only became 'futurist eschatology' when the realities of the present proved to be not as ideal as the pro-Davidic Jerusalem priesthood had in the first flush of enthusiasm conceived them to be. The attitude then became 'well, it is not quite the Kingdom of God yet, but it soon will be'. Prophetic visions of 'the Golden Age' and 'the Day of Yahweh' thus began to appear.[8] The other idea was that of God as 'the Lord of History'. God is working his purpose out, as year succeeds to year' is the compact expression of this notion, and it leads for christians to the assertion

[7] See 'Myth, Legend and History', in *The Beginning of the Promise, Eight Lectures on Genesis*, S. B. Frost, London, 1960, pp. 25–34; I accept, in its modern, modified form, the Graf-Wellhausen theory of Pentateuchal Sources.

[8] I justify this reading of Hebrew history, and this view of eschatology, here given very summarily, in my *Old Testament Apocalyptic*, the Fernley-Hartley Lecture for 1952, London, 1952, pp. 32–43.

that this programme culminates in his becoming incarnate as a man, that is, God became himself part of this world's history in the person of Jesus of Nazareth. Hence Christianity's particular concern with history and history-writing.

Christianity shares its basic view of history (though not of course the last-mentioned elaboration of it) with two other Hebrew-derived religions, Judaism and Islam. Each has developed the idea in accordance with its characteristics, and each has run into its own difficulties, but neither has placed the same emphasis, indeed reliance, on history as Christianity. It is not too much to say that intellectually Christianity stands or falls by its doctrine of history. Moreover, the christian idea of history is as influential in most christian circles today as ever it was; in fact, owing to the present popularity of so-called 'biblical theology', it is probably as warmly and uncritically embraced, even by theologians, as in any previous generation. Whereas other, non-Hebrew based religions are deprecatorily described as 'nature' religions, because they attempt to derive their knowledge of God from the physical order of the universe, Christianity designated itself as an 'historical' religion, because it claims to base itself upon a revelation given in and through history, and particularly the 'Christ-event', the man Jesus of Nazareth.

The formulation of this idea was in my view effected, as I have said, by a Judean priest of the David-Solomon period, the man (or men) whom we designate 'the Yahwist'. It was accepted and presupposed by the prophetic movement of the ninth to sixth centuries, but was most fully worked out by the seventh-century Deuteronomic School, both in that School's restatement of the teaching of Moses (in the book we call Deuteronomy) and also in its great series of histories, which we know as Joshua, Judges, Samuel and Kings. The later fifth-century Priestly School was rather less wholly-committed to this idea, while the strong and continuing Wisdom Tradition of the Old

Testament was hardly hospitable to the idea at all. Nevertheless, it has captivated many modern theologians, and ably led by the eminent Old Testament scholar von Rad, they have made it the one measuring-rod with reference to which all else in the Old Testament and indeed in the New Testament and in christian theology is to be judged.[9]

The problem which arises very acutely for this style of thinking is that actual events in time often do not very clearly support the theory that God is 'Lord of history' and that he is working his purpose out, slowly but surely, as year succeeds to year. As I have pointed out elsewhere, the post-exilic apocalyptic movement among the Jews arose very largely out of a despair of making the events of history fit the doctrine of history. When, as a result of the failure of the Bar-Kokhbah revolt, the Jews were disillusioned with apocalyptic also, they lapsed into an apathy with regard to history which can only be characterised by the cry 'How long, O Lord, how long?' With the recent successes of Zionism, however, the old Hebrew view of history

[9] 'The history of tradition has taught us in a new way to see in the three gigantic works of the Hexateuch, the Deuteronomistic History, and the Chronicler's History, the most varied forms of the presentation of God's history with Israel in its different strata. It has also shown how Israel was at all times occupied with the task of understanding her history from the point of view of certain interventions by God, and how what God had rooted in history presented itself in different ways in every age. . . . A theology which attempts to grasp the content of the Old Testament under the heading of various doctrines (the doctrine of God, the doctrine of man, etc.) cannot do justice to these credal statements which are completely tied up with history, or to this grounding of Israel's faith upon a few divine acts of salvation, and the effort to gain an ever new understanding of them.' Preface to von Rad's *Old Testament Theology*, Vol. I, E. T., New York and Edinburgh, 1962, pp. v–vi. For a fairly typical christian exposition of the New Testament and of the theological ideas deriving from it, we may turn to Bishop Stephen Neill's very thoughtful little book, *The Eternal Dimension*, London, 1963, pp. 69–70: 'Secondly, the Fourth Gospel introduces us to a very definite view of the nature of history. . . . As the writer of the Fourth Gospel understands the purpose of God, the glory of Christ . . . forms the central section of history; . . . but if this is true, and if the revelation of Christ is central, then no part of history is mere history. . . . There is no "mere history"; every human being is part of the history of God's love story with the human race.'

is gaining ground amongst the jewish people once more. Wilfred Cantwell Smith has very acutely diagnosed the present malaise of Islam as springing from a similar clash between the muslim belief in Allah as shaping history to Islam's benefit, a view largely upheld by the events of the seventh through to the fifteenth christian centuries, and the contradiction which that dogma has received from the tide of events since the emergence of christian Western Europe as the dominating power in human society, and particularly over the lands where Islam has been the major religion. Not a single muslim country, it should be recalled, has been free from that domination until the confused times of our own days. Indeed a great deal of the present unrest in the Middle East and in India arises from the need for muslim states to achieve political success in order to justify to themselves and to others the traditional muslim view of history—which is basically the Hebrew view that God is at work in history achieving his eternal purposes for those who are loyal to him.[10]

In our own time, the strain of upholding the Hebrew or biblical view of history has made itself felt in christian thought also. Here again we see the same retreat into apocalyptic-eschatological types of thought. This is particularly obvious in the case of the fundamentalist christian sects, such as the Seventh Day Adventists and the Jehovah's Witnesses, but it is also clearly discernible in the post-Depression and World War II theologians, as represented in America, for example, by Reinhold Niebuhr and his reaction against the progressivistic optimism of the Social Gospel movement, or more outspokenly by Karl Löwith who, though he has taught in the States, is more typically a German theologian. Löwith teaches that the

[10] For Judaism see my 'Apocalyptic and History', a paper read to the one hundredth General Meeting of the Society for Biblical Literature, New York, 1965, and published in *The Bible and Modern Scholarship*, ed. J. Philip Hyatt, Nashville, 1965, pp. 98–113. For Islam, see *Islam in Modern History*, Wilfred Cantwell Smith, Princeton, 1957, pp. 41 ff.

biblical view proclaims Jesus as the central event of history and that all so-called secular history is merely the historical interim which intervenes between the central event and the consummating conclusion. 'This "interim", he writes, 'i.e. the whole of history, is neither an empty period in which nothing happens nor a busy period in which everything may happen, but the decisive time of probation and final discrimination between the wheat and the tares.' Apart from this characterisation of being a time of judgement, he asserts, 'Historical processes as such do not bear the least evidence of a comprehensive and ultimate meaning. History as such has no outcome. There never has been and never will be an immanent solution of the problem of history, for man's experience is one of steady failure. Christianity, too, as a historical world religion, is a complete failure. The world is still as it was in the time of Alaric; only our means of oppression and destruction (as well as of reconstruction) are considerably improved and are adorned with hypocrisy.' When one recalls that, as a European, this man was a recipient of the Marshall Plan, one wonders whether to be grateful even for the parenthesis. But these two theologians are characteristic, in the one case soberly and in the other extravagantly, of the current tendency to retreat from the idea that God is presently at work in the current events of history, to the idea that he will intervene decisively at 'the end of the age', at the time of 'the Second Coming of Jesus', at 'the climax of history' or however it is phrased.[11]

It is disturbing that most of the theological discussion of

[11] For Niebuhr, see his *Children of Light and Children of Darkness*, New York 1944. The whole ethical discussion is strangely lacking in historical perspective, until on the last page, the God of history is brought in, *deus ex machina*: 'The last hope of Christian faith that the divine power which bears history can complete what even the highest human striving must leave incomplete, and can purify the corruptions which appear in even the purest aspirations, is an indispensable pre-requisite for diligent fulfilment of our historic tasks.' His able and serious study, *Faith and History*, New York, 1949, strongly rejects any idea of redemption in history, or even of judgment in history, and accepts only the judgment of history. Cf. p. 252. For Karl

history and its meaning, or lack of meaning, has gone on without reference to the professional historians' discussion of the same subject. As Paul Tillich commented: 'It is surprising how casually theological biblicists use a term like "history" when speaking of Christianity as a historical religion, or of God as "the Lord of History". They forget that the meaning they connect with the word "history" has been formed by thousands of years of historiography and philosophy of history.'[12] It is fitting, then, that we turn to what historians are saying among themselves about their own art—or perhaps we should say 'science', since one of the things for which most of them strongly contend is that history is a social science, and, incidentally, there-by declare themselves on one of the major issues of the debate.

Probably the most influential name is that of R. G. Collingwood, whose posthumous book *The Idea of History* was published in 1946.[13] The book reviews the writing of history from early days to the present—but not from the beginning since Hebrew historiography is dismissed on the curious grounds that in describing human activity it leaves a place for divine activity also. Collingwood also rejects the Mesopotamian chronicles on the additional (and almost as questionable) ground that the writer was retailing what he already knew, not what he had discovered as the result of research; but this latter charge, at least, cannot be levelled at the writers of the Deuteronomic Histories, since they surveyed several centuries and indeed often

Löwith, see his *Meaning in History*, Chicago, 1949. The passages cited are on pp. 184 and 191.

[12] *Systematic Theology*, Vol. I, p. 21.

[13] Edited by T. M. Knox, and published at Oxford. The book was certainly not helped by its editor's introduction, which, while explaining that it was put together from *disjecta membra* of unfinished manuscripts, leaves us in considerable doubt as to how far the book is expressive of Collingwood's mature thought, and indeed as to whether Collingwood ever gained a consistent and settled view of the matters discussed. Nevertheless, the book has been very influential because it encouraged historians to review their own activity with renewed seriousness.

cite their sources. I suspect that Collingwood was emotionally incapable of bringing the same kind of judgement to bear on biblical materials as on other ancient records, because like so many moderns he needed to demonstrate his emancipation from religious attitudes. He therefore dismissed the Bible as unworthy of serious study. An unbiased consideration would, however, quickly recognise that the deuteronomic historians composed their books to answer questions, that they researched to acquire their data, that they had a reverence for facts, and that they produced a continuous and self-consistent account of the four centuries from David to Zedekiah—and if Collingwood's definition of history excludes that great work, then I suggest that his definition is thereby shown to be too narrow and dogmatic. Only prejudice could lead a scholar to say that the Greeks wrote history and the Hebrews did not. On the contrary, we have to recognise that the Hebrews were conceiving and writing genuine history at least two hundred years before Herodotus, the so-called 'Father of History', was born.[14]

Nevertheless, Collingwood is undoubtedly right when he says that with Herodotus and Thucydides, the Greek writers of the fifth century B.C., something new emerged. They wrote histories of particular subjects, the former of the Persian Wars and the latter of the Peloponnesian War, and both wrote in purely humanistic terms. Moreover both wrote with a purpose in mind; Herodotus to explain how and why the Persians and Greeks were for so long and so persistently at war with each other, Thucydides to give such an account of the Greeks' internecine struggle as would offer guidance and wisdom for the future. Livy, writing in Rome at the turn of the christian era, saw all civilisation as one, that is, Roman, and tried to give such an account of Rome, its founding and its rise to greatness, as would make clear that that greatness derived from

[14] Or five hundred years, if we allow, as we ought, the recognition due to 'the Yahwist'.

the Romans' moral qualities. Tacitus, the historian of the early Principate, is even more moralistic: 'this attitude', writes Collingwood, 'leads Tacitus to distort history systematically by representing it as essentially a clash of characters, exaggeratedly good with exaggeratedly bad.'[15] What we need to note, however, is that the Greeks and the Romans (like the Hebrews) wrote their history with a purpose in mind. They too were telling the story of the past in such a way as to bring out a particular significance. Collingwood emphasises the persistence of these characteristics of universalism and providence in all later historiography right on into the christian centuries: 'Even in the Middle Ages nationalism was a real thing; but an historian who flattered national rivalries and national pride knew that he was doing wrong. His business was not to praise England or France but to narrate the *gesta Dei*. He saw history not as a mere play of human purposes, in which he took the side of his own friends, but as a process, having an objective necessity of its own . . . because God is provident and constructive, has a plan of his own with which he will allow no man to interfere. . . . The great task of medieval historiography was the task of discovering and expounding this objective or divine plan.'[16] Eusebius in the third century and Bossuet in the eighteenth were the first and latest in the long line of christian historiographers, and they were in no doubt as to the meaningfulness of the march of events.[17] In history God was working out the divine plan, and all creation was caught up in the movement towards the final and blessed consummation. The view is well summed up in Tennyson's reference to 'one far-off divine event, to which the whole creation moves'.

With the eighteenth century and 'the Age of the Enlightment', however, a new *motif* appeared in historiography. It is

---

[15] *The Idea of History*, p. 39.
[16] Ibid. p. 53.
[17] Perhaps we should include from our own times Kenneth Latourette. Cf. his *History of the Christian Church*, New York, 1953.

well illustrated by Gibbon's *Decline and Fall of the Roman Empire*. Here the nascent critical methods were used to write a history of Rome which upholds the pessimistic thesis that the motive force in history is human stupidity, and that barbarism and religion together triumph over the reason and culture of the best ages of the human spirit. His own best age Gibbon found in the time of the Antonine Emperors. But while Gibbon may differ from Bossuet in discerning what the motivating power in history is, he at least agrees with him in conceiving that the historian should detect and exhibit that power. This is also true of Kant, who published in 1784 an essay entitled *An Idea for a Universal History from the Cosmopolitan Point of View*, in which he set out that a universal history is a feasible idea, but must presuppose a plan, i.e. it should exhibit human rationality as coming progressively into being. For Hegel also, writing in the early 19th century, 'philosophical history' would again be a universal history of mankind, and would exhibit the progress from primitive times of the idea of freedom; but for Hegel this is no merely human process, but is rather a cosmic process, in which the world comes to realise itself in self-consciousness as spirit. Karl Marx, writing in the late nineteenth century, finds the motivating force in history to be nature, especially as it expresses itself in economic laws. For all of these writers, then, historiography sets out to produce an account of the past in such a way as to exhibit a particular meaning. That meaning may differ very greatly from that of the Judean priest in Jerusalem around one thousand BC, but they all follow him in seeing the historian's task as the discernment of a significance in the story of the past and its re-telling so as to make that significance apparent.

In the last quarter of the nineteenth century, however, a new development took place. Historians began to suspect all general schemes, and all the philosophies of history which lay behind them, as artificial and wholly speculative, deriving from the schememaker rather than from the data of history. They turned therefore to the determination of historical fact. 'The result was a vast increase of detailed historical knowledge, based to an unprecedented degree on meticulous and critical examination of evidence. This was the age which enriched history by the compilation of vast masses of carefully sifted material, like the calendars of close and patent rolls, the corpus of Latin inscriptions, new editions of historical texts and sources of every kind, and the whole apparatus of archeological research. The best historian, like Mommsen or Maitland, became the greatest master of detail. The historical conscience identified itself with an infinite scrupulosity about any and every isolated matter of fact. The ideal of universal history was swept aside as a vain dream, and the ideal of historical literature became the monograph.'[18] The greatest historian of the age was Leopold von Ranke, professor of history in the University of Berlin for nearly fifty years (1825–72). The historian's task, as he saw it, was to retell the past *wie es eigentlich gewesen*, 'as it actually happened'. This was 'scientific history'. It would lead, as Lord Acton supposed when planning the *Cambridge Modern History*, to the 'ultimate history'—the final, correct and uniquely true account of the past. He wrote: 'By the judicious division of labour we should be able to do it, and to bring home to every man the last document and the ripest conclusions of international research. Ultimate history we cannot have in this generation; but we can dispose of conventional history, and show the point we have reached on the road from one to the other, now that all information is within reach, and every problem has become capable of solution.'[19] There sounds the grand confidence of the English Victorian era, but that confidence has in our own period been shattered in historiography

[18] Collingwood, p. 127.
[19] *The Cambridge Modern History; the Origin, Authorship and Production*, Cambridge, 1907, p. 12. Cited E. H. Carr, *op. cit. infra*, note 23.

as in all things else. In the new century the Italian Croce began to teach that all history is 'contemporary history', meaning that all historiography depicts the past in terms of what interests the present and sees it through the spectacles of its own concerns. The point was made vividly by the American Carl Becker who in a thoughtful and stimulating article wrote in 1910 that 'the facts of history do not exist for any historian until he creates them and into every fact that he creates some part of his individual experience must enter.'[20] Professor Herbert Butterfield of Cambridge has given ample examples of the way in which historians determine not merely the past history of their people but also, by depicting for them their character and destiny, their future history also. He draws a contrast between the influence of the Whig interpretation of English history on the formulation of English character and aspirations with that of the nineteenth century German historians on German hopes for the future. He writes: 'Whatever we may feel about the defects of our own Whig interpretation of history, we have reason to be thankful for its influence on our political tradition, for it was to prove of the greatest moment to us that by the early seventeenth century our antiquarians had formulated our history as a history of liberty'. He also says: 'It would appear that German intellectual and public life in the nineteenth century succumbed to the leadership of academic thought and bowed before the professorial mind to a greater degree than was the case at that time in England. For their interpretation of human destiny, and of the role which their country had to play in the world, the intelligentsia were less guided by religion or tradition—or even perhaps by common sense—than ours; and they depended more on the picture which the academic historian provided. The historian in fact played an important part in the German national story in that period; for in effect it was he who said to the country:

[20] In an article in the *Atlantic Monthly*, October 1910, p. 528.

"See, *this* is your tradition, this is the line which the past has set for you to follow". . . . . The problem: "What is wrong with Germany?" has really culminated in the question: "What has been wrong with the German historical school?".'[21] Professor Peter Geyl of Utrecht has similarly drawn attention to the glorification of France and of the French Revolution which inspired the work of the nineteenth-century historian, Michelet, and which has since then coloured every Frenchman's idea of France. 'The humanitarian cosmopolitanism recommended by some', writes Geyl, 'does not appeal to (Michelet). *France* is what he preaches, the fatherland, the country blessed above all because it has vowed itself to the truths of the Revolution, and has been called to teach them to Europe for its happiness. This is the faith that the schools must inculcate into the minds of the coming generations. "The fatherland, first as dogma and principle; next as legend. Let the child be told, before all, that God has vouchsafed him the mercy of possessing this fatherland, which announced and wrote with its blood the law of divine equity and of fraternity, and that the God of the nations has spoken through France". In that sense, believing that France thinks for the world at large, Michelet is an internationalist. But for the practical politics of the moment, he teaches that England is the enemy, that every Frenchman must be warned not to count upon Europe, since he has no friend in the world but France. Also, that war is sure to come, and that France has no need to fear it, provided she firmly hold this faith.'[22] It is this view of French history which explains de Gaulle's messianism, his insistence on France being an independent nuclear power, his stedfast opposition to Britain's membership of the Common Market, his attempt to oust American influence from Europe, and his ambivalent attitude to the European community. To a very large extent, it is the

[21] *Man on His Past*, Cambridge, 1955, pp. 26–27.
[22] *Debates with Historians*, Gröningen and The Hague, 1955, p. 62.

nineteenth-century historian who is writing the policies of the twentieth-century statesman. And to these examples from Butterfield and Geyl, one may add that no single force has aroused a sense of national identity and destiny among the French Canadian people in the post-war years, so much as the writings of the historian of French Canada, the late Abbé Groulx.

History, then, is what the historian makes of it, and the insight of our own times is to recognise that he cannot help making something of it. He cannot hope to write 'objective' history. Referring to the nineteenth-century historian's obsession with the accumulation of facts, and his obstinate neglect of what to do with them, E. H. Carr says that he 'piously believed that divine providence would take care of the meaning of history if he took care of the facts. . . . The facts of history were themselves a demonstration of the supreme fact of a beneficent and apparently infinite progress towards higher things. This was the age of innocence, and historians walked in the Garden of Eden, without a scrap of philosophy to cover them, naked and unashamed before the god of history. Since then we have known Sin and experienced a Fall; and those historians who today pretend to dispense with a philosophy of history are merely trying, vainly and self-consciously, like members of a nudist colony, to recreate the Garden of Eden in their garden suburb. Today the awkward question can no longer be evaded.'[23]

It is now recognised, then, that every historian will in fact have a point of view, a set of basic assumptions which will colour and indeed condition all his work. Obviously, this 'philosophy of history', to grace it with a dignified term, or this inevitable bias, to derogate it with a perjurative term, must be in the case of each historian searched out, recognised and

[23] *What is History?*, London, 1961, p. 20. (The George Macaulay Trevelyan Lectures, delivered in the University of Cambridge, January–March, 1961.)

brought honestly into the open, not so much by the historian himself (who is not likely to be capable of this ruthless self-examination) as by his critics. Thus contemporary historians, if they find that a colleague has allowed his personal interests to intrude upon the data to the point of distortion, are quick and loud in their condemnation. This explains why Arnold Toynbee is popular with everyone except his professional colleagues. As early as 1946 when only the first six volumes of *A Study of History* had appeared, Pieter Geyl pointed out that Toynbee was not only guilty of imposing on history his vast scheme of twenty-one civilisations, and an arbitrary pattern of development and decline, but that he also selected his data and presented it in such a way as to persuade the unsuspecting general reader that the scheme and the philosophy arose out of the facts rather than were imposed upon them. Indeed, so brilliant was the presentation and so vast the erudition that many of the more discriminating were also liable to be deceived. With the publication of Volumes VII to X, and again with the appearance of the volume *Reconsiderations*, the professional historian's negative judgement has only been successively confirmed. Geyl speaks for all his colleagues when he writes '*A Study of History* is no history. The Student of History, as Toynbee calls himself, may know more history than I shall ever do, but he is no historian. He is a prophet. There has never been any love lost between prophets and historians.'[24]

[24] 'Toynbee the Prophet', *Journal of the History of Ideas*, 1955, reprinted in *Debates with Historians*, The Hague, 1955; the citation is from p. 171. He draws attention to 'the scornful reviews' of Toynbee's fellow professionals and in a footnote on p. 171 he mentions specifically A. J. P. Taylor, Geoffrey Barraclough, Hugh Trevor-Roper, and the anonymous reviewer in *The Times Literary Supplement*. But Geyl himself is no mere iconoclast; he has his own high concerns to maintain and he ends his discriminating essay by saying: 'If I have, in this essay, been primarily critical and destructive, the reason is not that, as I put it before, there is no love lost between prophets and historians. The prophet can be to the historian an exciting and moving subject. The reason is rather, not only that this prophet (Toynbee) usurps the name of historian, but especially that I regard his prophecy as a blasphemy

We can now see the historian's dilemma. He must not merely retail facts; in truth, as E. H. Carr shows brilliantly in his first lecture and particularly in his discussion of Stresemann's foreign policy, he *cannot* merely retail facts;[25] yet he must not make them the platform of his own prejudices nor prostitute them to become the sounding board of his own propaganda. He may, however, very legitimately—and indeed, he will quite inevitably—express in and through his treatment of his data his own interpretative principle. In this task, say the current philosophers of history, he can only try to steer skilfully between the Scylla of inchoate data and the Charybdis of contrived presentation, knowing that he will almost certainly be criticised by his colleagues for having veered too far on the one side or the other. For himself, he has to recognise that his whole exercise is to be in dialogue with his facts from the stance of his own philosophy of life.

This view of the historian's task cannot but be of the very greatest interest to christian scholars and theologians, since they have such a very definite stake in history. The traditional view has been, as we have seen, that whereas other religions were based on the uncertain vagaries of 'nature', Christianity was founded on the sure facts of 'history'. The distinction between 'natural theology' and 'revealed theology' was based primarily on this prior discrimination between 'nature' and 'history'. Revelation was neither simply a rational induction nor a mystical experience, but was an objective reality grounded in the sure facts of 'history'. This view goes back to the Judean priest of the tenth century BC who first adumbrated the Yahwist Pentateuchal Source; it was heavily reinforced by the seventh-

---

against Western Civilisation.' See also the transcript of his debate with Toynbee on the B.B.C. Third Programme January 4 and March 7, 1948, and Pitirim A. Sorokin's 'Toynbee's Philosophy of History', in *The Journal of Modern History*, September 1940, both reprinted in *The Pattern of the Past*, Boston, 1940.

[25] *What is History?*, London, 1961. See above, note 23.

century document, Deuteronomy; and by reason of the recent revival of 'biblical theology' has become one of the popular, largely unquestioned theological ideas of our time. Yet, as we have seen, when a modern historian looks at the Bible, this whole idea of a revelation in history dissolves itself into the unsubstantial bias of the biblical writers. 'Revelation' for our generation must be something read into history. It most certainly cannot be something derived from history.[26]

There are, I suggest, two conclusions of major importance for our enquiry to be drawn from this consideration of the nature of history and history writing. First, there is only one way in which the Old Testament can in this generation be

[26] This means that much current theology has become very dubious indeed. The following is not unfairly typical: 'the unique importance and value of the Bible is derived from the great and unique events it records. The things that God has done for man are recorded there, and give it a value above any other book. . . . The Scriptures which constitute for the Christian the evidence that God has acted to reveal himself, are of themselves inadequate to produce faith. . . . It is only when, in Cowper's phrase, 'The Spirit breathes upon the word and brings the truth to light' that revelation (*revelatio*) takes place . . . once the mind is interiorly persuaded by the Holy Spirit, the Bible attains a new realm and depth of meaning . . . the historical record of the Bible is properly intelligible only to those whose eyes have been opened' (*The Fulness of Time*, John Marsh, London, 1952, pp. 5–7). This is a position which can be (and is) equally adopted by a muslim with regard to the Qur'an and by a Latter Day Saint with regard to the Book of Mormon. However much it is buttressed with modern scholarship, it is basically obscurantist. The fact is that no protestant theologian has ever succeeded in establishing a unique let alone an absolute authority for the Bible, yet by a silent conspiracy highly-intelligent theologians write and think as if someone else, some otherwhere, has established this for them. (The best attempt is still C. H. Dodd's *The Authority of the Bible*, London, 1928, revised ed. 1938, but it nevertheless falls far short of what was expected of it.) This uncritical acceptance of the Bible also reveals itself in the teaching given in many if not most, theological colleges and seminaries; cf. the following from Charles Feilding's recent study *Education for Ministry*, Dayton, 1967, p. 12: 'I have been struck by how little attention is paid in many curricula to the canon of scripture and its authority. . . . Nevertheless "the Bible teaches" is an expression still used with astonishing abandon in circumstances where it is at least temerarious if not entirely without meaning". Dr Feilding was formerly Professor of Systematic Theology and Dean of Divinity at Trinity College, Toronto, and conducted his study on behalf of the American Association of Theological Schools.

allowed to speak significantly to us and that is by putting it
firmly back into its proper naturalistic setting. The Old Testament has to be viewed apart from the New; that is, apart from
those dogmatic concepts of the Old Testament which the New
Testament requires us to entertain, if we are truly to understand
the New Testament. In fact as christians we have to read the
Old Testament with double-vision: as an anthology of the
literature arising out of one nation's gallant attempt to become
a true community under God, and as the Word of God on
which the New Testament grounds itself. In the first view we
are called upon to note what considerations of morality, what
sense of inadequacy, what visions of further possibilities, what
mystical experiences of the individual, what sense of the wonder
of life, that gallant attempt led this amazing little people into.
The theme of the Old Testament is 'I will be their God and
they shall be my people' and from that theme proceded the
requirements of the Law and the ideals of the Prophets, the
spiritual growth-pains of the Psalmists, and the calm unhurried
reflections of the Wise Men. As an anthology of the human
spirit it is superb. Only the Greek literature can vie with it—
different in kind, far-more widely-ranging, out-shining the
Hebrew in brilliance but not achieving in my estimation an
equal depth of insight into what it means to be a community
and what it means to be a man. The Greek literature delights
us, the Hebrew challenges us. The Old Testament is one of
the high-tide marks of the inspiration of the spirit of life—
the Spirit of God, if you will—rising within the human mind.
As such it is a testimony to the nature of both God and man,
different in degree and in quality from all other such litera-
tures—the scriptures of Egypt, of India, of China, of Greece.
But not in kind. To take it out of its natural setting and ascribe
to it an inspiration and particularly an interpretation of history
which has a unique authority is to give it a value which on
closer examination it cannot sustain, and thereby to do this

truly amazing literature a disservice. We encourage a false expectation in the minds of honest and intelligent men and they are thereby prevented from appreciating its true and immense values. One of the first men to experience this disillusionment was Marcion and in doing so he made a great contribution to the evolution of Christianity. The other way of looking at the Old Testament is through the spectacles of the New Testament, and then we have to recognise the New Testament assessment of the Old as Scripture and as the unique Word of God, in order to understand the New. But that New Testament assessment is one I adopt for certain purposes; it cannot be one I permanently sustain in my attempt to interpret the human situation. As I try to understand who I am and what I should be seeking to become, the Old Testament has much to say which I find to be of particular significance and helpfulness, but there is also much which I put aside as irrelevant, immature and false. Great harm has been done through twenty centuries because we could not earlier arrive at this attitude of freedom of judgement with regard to the Old Testament. The Liberal-Protestant Reformation in the second half of the nineteenth century came as a blessed liberation of Western man—the literature of New England alone is testimony to that. But now the Old Testament can be seen for what it truly is—one of the most splendid achievements of the divinely-inspired human spirit. I worship on every one of its high hills, and I refresh myself beneath every one of its green trees.

The second major conclusion we draw from our consideration of history refers to the judgement we are to make on the significance of the past story of man: that is, the conclusion we are to reach with regard to history itself. Once the Old Testament is given its true value, its interpretation of history deserves careful re-consideration. We may rehearse the matter thus: man in his cultural evolution reached a state of society in which social and hereditary grouping began to take on a powerful significance for him. Family-type loyalties began to be expanded into tribal loyalties. In Israel (as in many other instances) a number of such tribes came together into an 'amphictyony', that is, a group of clans united by ties which were primarily religious. In the case of Israel, they believed themselves to be 'in covenant' with a god called Yahweh. They later conceived that this god was God and that he was active in the events of their history making of them a 'people' and giving them an identity, a land, a kingship and above all a law whereby they should live. The importance of this biblical view of Israelite history is not primarily whether they have or have not correctly interpreted the significance of their own history (they themselves came to see in due time some of the very great problems involved)[27] but rather that they had stumbled upon a clue to the interpretation of human history as a whole. To detect the physiological evolution of man during the past ten thousand years is not possible; to see it clearly in the evidence of the past two million years is very easy. To detect the spirit of God at work in the detail of the seven or so centuries[28] of Israelite history is a very debatable proposition but to see him at work in the whole sweep of human history from the slow first beginnings in the time of the Early Mousterians to the emergence of civilisation some six or seven thousand years ago and the more recent world-domination of the species is a much more defensible procedure. The importance of the Bible is that it first gave us this idea that history has a meaning. H. A. L. Fisher in his famous comment on the history of Europe said that he could see in it no particular significance; the answer is

[27] See my paper 'Apocalyptic and History', cited in note 10 above.

[28] The deuteronomic school applied their idea to the period from Abraham to the Exile, but in practical terms it was limited to the period from the twelfth to the sixth centuries B.C. (It is still argued whether, if Abraham was an historical figure, he should be placed in the nineteenth or the thirteenth century B.C. The Exodus is fairly firmly located, however, in the second half of the thirteenth century.)

surely that he was looking at a mass of too-crowded detail crammed into too short a period.[29] But when we stand back and survey even the past eight thousand years, we are much more justified in saying that this grand sweep of human history, as a part of the cosmic evolutionary process, is indeed significant and that in it, as in all evolution, we can see God, the Reason of the Universe, working his purposes out in time and in human affairs. Fisher himself said 'the fact of progress is written plain and large on the page of history', and the glory of the Old Testament is that it has given us the clue to an interpretation of history as a whole, which is consonant with the interpretation of the human situation suggested to us by our consideration of what we can learn about ourselves, and by our consideration of the natural order which is our environment.

To the historian, then, we must accord the same professional freedom as that which we gave to the biologist—the freedom to work at his discipline on a purely scientific, humanistic basis. As a professional, he must select, display, interpret his data without reference to God. But not as if God were not. At times he, too, must cease to be a professional and must become again a whole man, and must stand back and see the total story of mankind, and then, like the rest of us, be awed at the thought of the slow, deliberate but meaningful activity, which works in

[29] Though he did draw from his study a conclusion of very great significance—that development is neither uniform nor automatic. 'Men wiser and more learned than I have discerned in history a plot, a rhythm, a predetermined pattern. These harmonies are concealed from me. I can only see one emergency following upon another as wave follows wave, only one great fact with respect to which, since it is unique, there can be no generalisation, only one safe rule for the historian: that he should recognise in the development of human destinies the play of the contingent and the unforeseen. This is not a doctrine of cynicism and despair. The fact of progress is written plain and large on the page of history; but progress is not the law of nature. The ground gained by one generation may be lost by the next. The thoughts of men may flow into channels which lead to disaster and barbarism.' H. A. L. Fisher, *A History of Europe*, Preface to Vol. I: *Ancient and Mediaeval*, London, 1935.

and through human affairs and which endows those affairs with an end-directedness, pointing forward to a destiny as yet unknown. God is indeed working his purpose out, and I have to try to understand that purpose, and to latch on to it, if I can, the little endeavour of my own being, so that I become part of the meaning of the universe at large.[30]

The christian Bible, however, has two Testaments, and the New Testament confronts me with one particular historical fact as being of paramount importance. The New Testament interprets the life and death of Jesus of Nazareth, as having a unique significance, in that, in this man, God became a human being, one of ourselves, a fact of human history. If this is true I have to recognise in Jesus a lordship and an authority which is indeed unique, and in seeking to understand my existential situation accept him as a teacher and guide. It is therefore a proposition which I must consider very closely.

[30] Since writing this chapter, I have been much encouraged by reading the essay 'The Historian's Dilemma' by J. H. Plumb, Reader in Modern History at Cambridge, in the volume edited by him under the title *Crisis in the Humanities*, London, 1964. He gives a very informative account of recent schools of historiography and then says: 'So there we have them. The idealists insisting that history is merely a present world, ever changing, never static; the academic positivists burrowing like boll-weavils in the thickets of facts, mindless, deliberately, of purpose and meaning outside the orbit of their own activity; the public prophets using pseudo-science to justify a repetitive, cyclical interpretation of history, and the littérateurs pre-occupied with evocation and exercise of the imagination. The result is nihilistic and socially impotent. All are equally guilty I think of wilfully rejecting the one certain judgement of value that can be made of history and that is *the idea of progress*. If this great human truth were once more to be frankly accepted, the reasons for it, and the consequences of it, consistently and imaginatively explored and taught, history would not only be an infinitely richer education, but also play a much more effective part in the culture of western society.' The italics are Dr Plumb's.

Chapter Six

JESUS OF NAZARETH

I AM at this point in my enquiry faced with a question as to how I should proceed. Should I attempt to deal with Jesus as a fact of history, or should I assess him as the Christ of faith, the one urged upon me as the answer to the needs of my existential human situation? I have decided to choose the latter course, since if it were not for the claims made by the christian religion on behalf of Jesus, he would not be a subject for our present discussion. Nevertheless, those very claims will lead us back to a consideration of Jesus himself, and to a discussion as to whether he can in fact sustain the claims made by the Church on his behalf.

I shall attempt, therefore, first to say what the christian estimate of Jesus has over the centuries come to be; secondly, to see how far that estimate is compatible with, indeed, can be expressed in, the terms of modern concepts; and only thereafter and thirdly how far and on what grounds that estimate may be justified. The justification for that second step is that what I think about Jesus must be able to form part of the same thought-world as computers and neutrons and nucleic acids, if it is to be relevant and meaningful to our present age. Some theologians may criticise this as a methodology which accommodates 'the Gospel' to 'the world', instead of demanding that 'the world' conform to 'the Gospel', but, as I see it, I have to take account of the facts of the present situation. The scientific, technological thought-world is undeniably with us, and what I think on any subject, but especially on religion must be compatible with and expressive in the language of its concepts. As will be seen, I believe the christians of the first centuries set us in this respect a very good example. Nevertheless the third and final question is the all-important one. When I have determined what it is that christians want to say about Jesus, and when I have considered how far what they want to say can be said in the language of our own day, the question still remains: do I want to say that about him? If so, on what grounds? As I stand on a shrinking planet in an expanding universe trying to make sense of the human situation, do I find that Jesus has anything particularly significant to say to me about God, my relations with others, my personal significance? These are questions which I must obviously seek to face as honestly as I can.

The story of the growth and formulation of christian belief in Jesus offers a richness of materials and a challenge of intellectual interest, sufficient for many men to have made it the absorbing subject of a life-time study. It begins with the enthusiasm of some Galilean villagers and fisher-folk for an itinerant preacher. It moves to the devoted loyalty of his immediate followers who even when they had seen him executed, refused to believe he was dead and were themselves prepared to die rather than refrain from propagating their faith. It was a matter at this early stage of a conviction that Jesus was and is the one designated by God to be his agent in bringing history to its great climax and consummation—he is, to use the technical term, God's 'Anointed'. The term implies he has been designated (originally literally by anointing) for this particular task; in Hebrew it is 'the Messiah' and in Greek it is 'the Christ'.

One of the concomitant titles of the Messiah was 'God's

Son', a loose, vague phrase, used at various times of Israel as a nation, or of Israel's reigning Davidic King, or even of a very good man. We ourselves still talk occasionally of 'the great Protestant divines of the eighteenth century'. But the early christians began to put into the term 'Son of God' a new and fuller meaning: that Jesus was uniquely related to God in an essential sense. This new meaning is already becoming evident in such New Testament phrases as 'the only Son, who is in the bosom of the Father', and 'in him all the fullness of God was pleased to dwell'. These ideas were accompanied by the notion that Jesus was originally God and condescended to become man. This is already recognisable in a passage from Paul's Letter to the Philippians, in which speaking of Jesus he writes: 'who, though he was in the form of God, did not count equality with God a thing to be grasped, but emptied himself, taking the form of a servant, being born in the likeness of men'. These are all first-century statements, the last (presuming that it is genuinely Pauline) originating within thirty years of Jesus' death.[1]

The early christian centuries were pre-occupied with one of the most, if not the most, prolonged intellectual discussions which have ever engaged the mind of man. From at least the second century through to the fifth, the best minds of the time grappled with the question: 'How could Jesus be truly God and truly man at one and the same time?' Throughout the varying fortunes of the long debate as tempers hardened and positions were adopted, and proposals were labelled 'heresies' and bitterly attacked, and even when divisions began to occur in the original community and christian would no longer recognise or consort with christian, the fundamental objectives of the Church remained consistently clear: on the one hand, Jesus must be shown to be fully human, since only a full and normal member of the human race could truly share in the human

[1] John 1:18; Colossians 1:19; Philippians 2:6.

situation; on the other hand, if he was not to be just one more vague visionary, one more hopeful speculator, guessing out of the common ignorance who God is and what his intentions are, then he must be directly and authentically from God, he must be 'on the Godward side of reality'; not merely an intermediary between God and man, but God himself. As the mediaeval hymn expressed it:

> He sent no angel to our race,
> Of higher or of lower place,
> But wore the robe of human frame
> Himself, and to this lost world came.

It is noteworthy that the motivation of the debate was highly practical and not abstractly intellectual; mankind was believed to be in a desperate position, a situation of doom and despair, and in urgent need of a Saviour; but only one who was God-man could effectively fulfil that rôle. The problem was, then, to state, in some way which was acceptable to reason, how Jesus could be God and man at one and the same time.

As an early off-shoot of this debate there developed the recognition that if Jesus was God he was clearly not the sole possessor of the divine power of the universe. During his human existence, life was still being maintained by a transcendent power immanent in all things; to put it simply, God was clearly still running the universe while Jesus was being born, growing up, teaching and dying in Palestine. Moreover, the early christians were conscious of a dynamism at work in their movement and in their individual lives which again seemed to them a separate and in some sense distinct activity of the divine. They were thus led to the trinitarian view of the divine life of the universe: that in the mystery of the Divine Being (and they were in no doubt, for all their bold speculations, that God was a mystery, to be approached even in thought with head bowed and feet unshod) there were three centres of consciousness (their term *hypostasis* does not have the insularity of our term 'person') which while they were one in identity were nevertheless three in activity. It was a beautiful, poetic and mythopoeic piece of abstract reasoning, which dealt satisfyingly with all the elements in the situation, like a scientific theory which is accepted because it accounts comprehensively for all the evidence. The doctrine of the trinitarian being of God has remained since those early days as the crown of christian theology, nobly satisfying the deepest needs of christian worship. It ranks with Plato's Theory of Ideas and with the nuclear theory of the structure of matter as a supreme example of man's speculative powers. Nor is there anything irrational or absurd in the basic thought. We are very familiar with levels of being—the existence of a stone, the botanical life of a plant, the biological life of a fish, the quasi-intelligent life of a dog, the mature personality of a man. There is nothing irrational in presuming that the divine level of being must transcend our own in this ascending series, and that whereas we know the personal level of being as possessing a singularity of consciousness, another level of being could enjoy a plurality of consciousness, even though we ourselves necessarily cannot imagine what that level of being would be like to experience. In saying this, I am in no way establishing or seeking to establish the 'truth' of the christian doctrine of the Trinity; I am saying that it is compatible with, and not obnoxious to, the rationality of the universe as we know it. I myself would describe it as the christian 'myth' or 'model' of God, a statement which accommodates all the factors in the situation which arises if one accepts the basic christian premise that Jesus is, in some sense which other men are not, God in human form, but which obviously none of us is in a position to affirm as an ontological statement. It is not, in other words, a scientific description but it is a perceptive and pregnant metaphor, which has revealed its quality in christian worship through twenty centuries.

It has to be remembered that the classical doctrine of the person of Jesus was hammered out at a time when the categories of speculative thought were wholly Greek. Being was thought of as a 'substance', a 'something', whereas we will probably be described by some subsequent culture as thinking of being as an on-going experience. A substance was thought of as having a 'nature', a pattern of behaviour or series of attributes, as it were. Clearly, Jesus had a physical, human body[2] and the final solution arrived at was that Jesus had in the one *hypostasis* (which is to be equated with what we call 'personality') two 'natures' the one being of the same 'substance' (*ousia*) as God, the other being of the same 'substance' as mankind. He had two wills, a divine will and a human will, but the human delighted to be in harmony with the divine. It may seem to us a curiously materialistic analysis of a living personality, and indeed whether it really adequately protected the belief in Jesus' true humanity is very much open to question, but of the seriousness of the intention there can be no doubt. This view of the historical person Jesus of Nazareth became, and for that matter still is, christian orthodoxy. We should give the early christians full credit for recognising the need to state clearly their belief in Jesus in the rational terms of their day, so that their faith might be coherent with their understanding of all else in the human situation. It is significant that they strove for the rationality of the christian faith even at the cost of controversy and dissension.

Christians of our own day can hardly be given similar credit. We no longer accept the Greek view of personality as a 'substance', a 'thing'. If there are two substances, one can conceive that they mix or that they intermingle or that they fuse, or

---

[2] An early attempt to solve the problem by saying that Jesus was wholly divine and only 'appeared' as a man, an apparition not a real body, was quickly and contemptuously dismissed.

that they remain in close juxta-position, quite separate, side by side in the same entity, rather like an emulsion—all these ideas with respect to the two 'natures' of the God-man Jesus were tried out in the christological debate. But current concepts do not conceive of personality as a 'thing' and we in our generation cannot think of the person of Jesus in these quasi-physical terms. Yet we have done very little towards the creation of a new understanding of the person of Jesus. W. E. Montefiore has said that until the human sciences give us a clearer concept of human personality, it is unlikely that we will be able to state satisfactorily a christological theory.[3] That is not wholly true; the fact is that we already have, as we have seen, a good working theory of human personality, and our ideas about Jesus must at least be consonant with that theory.

As we saw in the second chapter, the modern view begins with the physical organism of the body, the complexity of the cortex, the neurochemistry and neuroelectricity of the brain, the establishment of circuit-patterns, the creation of concepts, the attainment of self-conceptualisation, the emancipation of mind from the mechanistic processes of the cortex, and the slow, educatory growth of personality, which is a stream of consciousness possessing memory and able (at least in some small but crucial measure) to make choices and decisions relating to the future. Personality for us derives from the physical organism and we are unlikely ever to go back on that. The germinated ovum in Mary's womb developed into the physical organism which was her child, and that organism developed its own centre of consciousness, which was Jesus. Any other centre of consciousness which had any different origin would in our terms clearly be 'not Jesus'. A 'two-nature' theory of personality is, as I see it, quite ruled out by our basic understanding of what personality is. The question

[3] 'Towards a Christology for Today' in *Soundings*, ed. A. R. Vidler, Cambridge, 1962, p. 155, note 2.

arises, then, whether it is indeed possible to state the christian estimate of Jesus in terms compatible with contemporary ways of thinking.

When the christian says 'God become man', he is wanting, I suggest, to say two things. First, that God can have full sympathy with our moral and mental struggles, full understanding for what it means to be human, because he has literally become 'one of us':

> *Touched with a sympathy within,*
> *He knows our feeble frame;*
> *He knows what sore temptations mean,*
> *For he hath felt the same.*

The other thing the christian is concerned to affirm is that Jesus was something new in human history: that he was God breaking into human existence. Jesus brought a new understanding of God and a new knowledge of his intentions with respect to the human race, and it is a revelation we can accept as fully authoritative because he really does know—he *is* God.

As regards providing within the context of modern thought for the former assertion, I see less difficulty. We all know that the insularity of human identity can be transcended. When we read a good novel, or even more when we see a good play, we identify with the main character, and live his life and enter into his emotions and agonise over his crises to the point where we have experienced his experiences. In the parent-child relationship a more persistent identification of one person with another is again familiar to us. A mother knows just how her little daughter feels towards her favourite doll; a father identifies with his small son facing a large school for the first time. I can conceive that God could deeply share, to the point of an even closer identification, in the emergent sensations of the embryo in Mary's womb, in the experiences of the boy growing up in Nazareth, in the years of pondering in youth and manhood, in the moment of decision on the banks of Jordan, in the utter dedication to ministry, and even in the merciless sufferings of death by pain and thirst and exhaustion which crucifixion entails. God, I can conceive, could identify with Jesus experiencing what it means to be a man. God would have 'become man' and Jesus would be rightly called Immanu-el, 'God with us'. A concept of personal intercourse so close as to be described as 'identification' or 'symbiosis' is compatible with our psychological categories, and would I believe, allow a christian to say all that he needs to say under that head.[4] What is special about Jesus is that he is the one with whom God chose to identify.

But will that identification-concept provide for 'the irruption of the divine' into human history, which the traditional christian understanding of the incarnation has always intended to assert? Not, I think, until we have added a further thought. The only way, as far as I can presently see, for a christian accepting the modern account of human personality, to think of Jesus as 'God become man' in this second sense is to accept fully the biblical assertion that man was made 'like God' (in his 'image', is the biblical term)[5] and to conceive that, because God is the life of the universe, when that life expresses itself most fully and perfectly in a human person, that person is divine, he is

---

[4] Possibly not all that he *desires* to say, but in theology as in all else we have to be satisfied if our *needs* are met. In this brief reference to the great christological debate I have ignored the difference (and problems arising from the difference) between the Greek terms *ousia, physis, hypostasis* and *prosopon*, and their near but not identical Latin equivalents *substantia, natura*, and *persona*. For a simple account of the major theories, see my brother's little book, *This Jesus*, Eric George Frost, London, 1959, and for a discussion of recent christological teaching see *Son of Man, Son of God*, Eric George Jay, Montreal, 1965. Dr Jay is Professor of Historical Theology and my successor as Dean of the Faculty of Divinity at McGill.

[5] Genesis 1:26-27.

God.[6] There has always been a strain in christian teaching which
has recognised the element or quality of the divine in every
man, starting (as so many good christian ideas do) from a
misunderstanding of an Old Testament text: 'I said, you are
gods'.[7] The idea has been preserved in the teaching and
liturgies of the Eastern Orthodox tradition: 'He became man
that we might become God'.[8] It comes out again in Bishop
Wordsworth's great hymn on the ascension:

> *He has raised our human nature,*
> *In the clouds at God's right hand,*
> *There we sit in heavenly places,*
> *There with Him in glory stand;*
> *Jesus reigns adored by angels,*
> *Man with God is on the throne,*
> *Mighty Lord, in Thine Ascension,*
> *We by faith behold our own!*

It has not been a prominent thought in the christian tradition,
and it has not been beloved by protestant theologians, but it is
part of the fullness of christian thought, and it may be that if
christians are to be able to express in modern terms what they

[6] Dean Jay discusses sympathetically if critically the attempts of modern
theologians such as Donald Baillie, Paul Tillich, Dietrich Bonhoeffer, J. A. T.
Robinson, W. R. Matthews, W. E. Montefiore to state the christian doctrine
of incarnation in contemporary terms. They all abandon the ontological
category of *substance* (though W. R. Matthews tries perhaps to abandon it
and retain it, at one and the same time) and they all move into a moral or
qualitative assessment of Jesus' divinity: 'Because Christ was utterly and
completely "the man for others", because he *was* love, he was "one with the
Father", because "God is love" ' (J. A. T. Robinson, *Honest to God*, p. 76.).
This, I believe, given our present concepts, is inevitable. But a qualitative
assessment without reference to the problems of personality-structure is, I
submit inadequate, and leaves us with many of our most cogent questions
unanswered.

[7] Psalm 82:6.

[8] Cf. Athanasius, *De Incarnatione* in *Nicene and Post-Nicene Fathers*,
Vol. IV, p. 54.

have always tried to affirm about Jesus, this line of thought will have to be re-explored. In Jesus, we will have to say, the difference between man and God is transcended; in Jesus' human maturity, God is expressing himself fully in human personal terms. His uniqueness lies in just that uniqueness which (as Professor Wald insisted) is the remarkable characteristic of all personality—that he was Jesus, and not John or Caiaphas, but was this man with these endowments and with these experiences. Furthermore, we will add, his peculiar significance lies not only in the fact that it was his life which God chose to share in a fullness of sympathy which we may call 'identification', but also in the fact that it was through his life that God expressed himself fully in terms of human personality. He was thus (to use the Old Testament term) the one 'elected' to be Messiah, the one chosen to be God's Son. This, I suggest, expresses about Jesus as God-come-among-us, all that a christian should properly be concerned to say of him, and is consonant with the modern concept of personality.[9]

It may be objected that this view reduces Christianity to a mere naturalism and that it does not provide for the concept of God breaking into human life, the divine irruption into history. My suggestion is that we are being somewhat misled at this point by our metaphors—that there is nothing intrinsically superior or more advantageous in conceiving of God 'breaking into' history than to conceive of him 'arising out of' history. On the contrary, given our understanding of the uniformity of nature (an understanding which, as we have seen, is integral to the world-view of the natural sciences) the latter is the more meaningful and therefore more attractive concept.

[9] This view does not envisage (as many will think it should) that the identity of God with Jesus was unique in kind, as well as in degree, but it has never been needful, as Thomas Aquinas saw, to assert the unique in the sense of unrepeatable character of the Incarnation. He allowed that in christian theory God could become incarnate again in another man than Jesus. Cf. H. R. Mackintosh, *The Person of Christ*, Edinburgh, 1912, p. 229.

The first metaphor arises out of a lingering remnant of our discarded concept of 'miracle', i.e. a divine interference with the ordinary course of nature to produce the desired end quickly and conveniently. We are all small children at heart, and we all want the pumpkin to turn magically into a carriage, and Cinderella to become in a moment a beautiful princess, and for plain water to be transformed into wine, but we have learnt that God has more respect for the orderliness of the universe, and just does not do that kind of thing. So, too, the incarnation itself must not be reduced to God's greatest conjuring trick, his most amazing piece of magic. Rather, if God becomes man in this kind of a universe it will be by the slow process of the natural order, whereby one man emerges with such maturity and such excellence of being that he is in terms of a human personality the expression of God himself. Of such a man it might truly be said 'He that has seen him, has seen the Father'. We have to grow up in our thinking and recognise the deeper, maturer wisdom that inheres in the slow growths of evolution, and understand that the true miracle is the emergence of Jesus as a fully-mature human being from the lowly beginnings of *australopithecus* and the long line of hominids and lesser creatures which preceded him. I suggest, then, that if we conceive of Jesus as truly man, fully, maturely man, we may recognise him as the expression of God in human terms and may rightly call him Immanu-el, 'God with us'. I also suggest that in these two thoughts of the historical identification of God with the man Jesus, and the emergence in Jesus of that true humanity which is the expression of the divine in human terms, we have at least begun to conceive of the incarnation in modes of thought which are consonant with the contemporary understanding of the world-order, of personality, and of history.[10]

[10] In my own mind I have tagged these ideas 'symbiosis', God living with Jesus, and 'diabiosis', God living through Jesus. Some critics will

As I ponder these matters, I am conscious that they are leading up to the truly decisive ones for the christian. Starting as all men must from the existential, human situation, a man can find his way to a personal interpretation of himself and to a theistic interpretation of the universe in which he finds himself to be. But these convictions do not make him a christian. What distinguishes him as a christian, and endues his life with a particular character and significance, is his estimate of Jesus of Nazareth, and his commitment of loyalty to him as the Christ, the manifestation of God in terms of human personalitv. The questions I have to ask myself, then, are these: is there that in Jesus which makes me ready to share in the christian estimate of this man, and to accord him that lordship which christians have freely offered to him? Do I find in him a maturity of humanity and an insight into the nature of God which would lead me to say 'If an incarnation of God in the terms in which we have discussed it, has taken place, it was in the life of this man, Jesus of Nazareth'?

---

affirm that I have retreated to the position of Matthew Tindal and his *Christianity as Old as the Creation* (1730) or even of John Toland and his *Christianity not Mysterious* (1696). Others again will say that the view I have expressed is unchristian because it is compatible with unitarian ways of thought. But anyone seeking to be honest about the christian faith must be as little deterred by these theological resorts to the dubious charge of 'guilt by association' as was Luther in his debate with Eck, when the latter sought to overthrow Luther's position by showing that it was essentially that of the condemned heretic, John Hus. 'Very well, then' said Luther in effect 'I agree with John Hus'. I would prefer to say that I would now feel no incongruity in finding myself in the same church as one who could not subscribe to the so-called Athanasian creed or who formally described himself as a unitarian. These gross labels are very inadequate to describe the extremely subtle variations and gradations of belief and faith. Others again will say that I have reverted to a fundamentally 'adoptionist' christology, or that I am suggesting an apotheosis rather than an incarnation: Jesus was generated an organism, developed into a person, matured into a true man, and thus became God. I would have to agree that this is not a distortion of my thinking—and again say that I am not deterred by labels. Adoptionist and apotheotic views may have been very wrong in the thought-world of the Greek categories; they may I suggest, be very right in the evolution-dominated context of our own thinking.

Even to ask these questions implies that I have dependably accurate knowledge of him, but this proposition has been very severely challenged in our time. Ever since Albert Schweitzer wrote his damaging book *The Quest of the Historical Jesus* the thought has haunted the protestant community: do we each and everyone of us build a dream-figure of Jesus, reading the facts of his life to conform with our notions of what he ought to have been, and turning the thrust of his teaching to make it support our own preconceived ideas of what life should be? While deluding ourselves that we are his followers and servants, do we in fact make him serve us and our selfish ends? I called Schweitzer's book damaging, and indeed it was destructive of much false piety and of many false estimates of Jesus, and was a truly necessary piece of work; but it was damaging in that *any* estimate of Jesus is now open to the same criticism. Schweitzer presented his own understanding of Jesus, but this did not win universal approval by any means, and the idea was left that Jesus was in fact unknowable: the materials available to us are too scanty, the clues to his character too enigmatic. The situation has not been improved by the radical scepticism on this point of the greatest figure in New Testament studies in the present century, Rudolph Bultmann, my own teacher at Marburg thirty years ago. He was a dominating figure then, but his stature has grown with the years. Moreover, increasing reliance upon 'form criticism' in the study of the records of Jesus' life and teaching has thrown still further doubt upon the authenticity of the information available to us, until now the position has been reached where responsible New Testament scholars are saying in effect that the historical person Jesus of Nazareth is lost for ever, and in his place we have only the creation of the Early Church, a figure designed to meet the needs and fulfil the aspirations of the second generation of christians, but having little likeness to historical truth.

An able and representative exponent of these views is

Norman Perrin who begins his book *Rediscovering the Teaching of Jesus* with a clear declaration of his assumptions, which he affirms to be the assured results of contemporary scholarship. We cannot but recall how often 'the assured results' of one generation have been sweepingly rejected by the next, but Dr Perrin certainly stands in an established tradition of meticulous scholarship and is of unchallengeable honesty. He writes: 'The early church made no attempt to distinguish between the words the earthly Jesus had spoken and those spoken by the risen Lord through a prophet in the community, nor between the original teaching of Jesus and the new understanding and re-formulation of that teaching reached in the catechesis or parenesis of the Church under the guidance of the Lord of the Church. The early Church absolutely and completely identified the risen Lord of her experience with the earthly Jesus of Nazareth and created for her purposes, which she conceived to be his, the literary form of the gospel, in which words and deeds ascribed in her consciousness to both the earthly Jesus and the risen Lord were set down in terms of the former'. He continues, 'when we read an account of Jesus giving instruction to his disciples, we are not hearing the voice of the earthly Jesus addressing Galilean disciples in a Palestinian situation but that of the risen Lord addressing christian missionaries in a Hellenistic world . . . there may have been a faint echo of the voice of the earthly Jesus . . . but . . . fine tuning indeed will be needed to catch it.'[11] It would be presumptuous in a few lines to attempt to answer what is cogently argued through a whole book, but I have to recognise that if this statement of the situation has to be accepted then Christianity, as far as I can see, has been shown to be false at the one point where it most

[11] Norman E. Perrin, *Rediscovering the Teaching of Jesus*, London, 1967, p. 15; 'catechesis' is largely the doctrinal teaching and 'parenesis' the moral teaching of the christian community. Dr Perrin is presently Professor in the Department of New Testament in the Divinity School of the University of Chicago.

needs to be true. If Christianity claims that God expressed himself in terms of human personality, and entered into human history in the person of Jesus of Nazareth, and then scholars tell us that the life he lived as man is historically lost to us, then the whole incarnation-event has surely been reduced to an exercise in futility. The idea of incarnation, which is central to Christianity, has become irrelevant to history, and therefore as far as I am concerned quite untenable.

Dr Perrin is aware of this problem and relates in his last chapter how he and those scholars, who share his views, attempt to meet it. On their general approach I have to comment that they appear to have a predilection for philosophy which is out of proportion to their respect for history or their feeling for the natural sciences. They pass subtly from a fact, a datum, whether of history or of the natural order, to a concept, an idea, whether in the mind of the early church or of the historic church, without any sense of the profound difference involved. Thus Dr Perrin attempts to defend christian worship of Christ as God by saying that we have three kinds of knowledge of Jesus: historical knowledge (knowledge of the historical figure Jesus of Nazareth as a fact of past time) historic[12] knowledge (knowledge of Jesus as a figure of the past who has become significant to us in our own time) and faith-knowledge, i.e. knowledge at the level of religious faith and commitment. He then says: 'So, for the christian, it is possible to say "Christ died for my sins in accordance with the scriptures". This, however, is a statement of faith not of history in the normal sense. ... None of this is history in the post-Enlightenment sense of that word; nor is it dependent on the manner or mode

[12] This refers to the difference of idea expressed in German by the two words *Historie* and *Geschichte* for both of which 'history' in English has to do service. Thus a German can talk of *der historische Jesu* (the 'historical' Jesus) and *der geschichtliche Christus*, (the 'historic' Christ) the one a fact of past history, the other a changing and developing concept through many ages reaching up into our own.

of the death of Jesus, only on the fact that it happened. The value here ascribed to that death is not ascribed to it because of what Jesus did, but because of what God is regarded as having done. The death of Jesus is not efficacious because he died nobly, or because he showed confidence in God, but because the cross is believed to have fulfilled the purpose of God. That Jesus died nobly or showed confidence in God are historical statements, subject to the vicissitudes of historical research, but that his death fulfilled the purpose of God in regard to 'my sins' is certainly not such a statement, and it lies beyond the power of the historian, even though, as a christian he might believe it.'[13] My disagreement with this reasoning is that, honest as it intends to be, it has passed the borderline of sophistication and has become special pleading: an attempt to dispense with the historical Jesus and yet retain a doctrine of atonement attached to his death. If evidence ever came to light that Jesus resisted arrest, tried every way he could to escape the charge brought against him, pleaded for acquittal and went to death blaspheming against God who had let him down and cursing all mankind, it would have become impossible for a christian to continue saying: 'Christ died for my sins according to the scriptures.' It would be impossible to characterise that death as God notably at work in human suffering, and it certainly would not conform to the established biblical pattern of suffering obedience. Such a death would not in fact have 'fulfilled the scriptures'. If again the historian produced evidence to show that Jesus did not die by crucifixion *sub Pontio Pilato*, but in fact lived to a ripe old age because a substitute had been smuggled into his place, again it would be impossible for a christian to continue saying: 'Christ died for my sins according to the scriptures'. There is in that 'historic' statement an 'historical' element which cannot be eliminated.

In other words, while Dr Perrin's distinction between the

[13] *Op. cit.* p. 237.

three kinds of knowing may be useful for certain purposes, it must not be allowed to obscure the point (equally an insight of post-Enlightenment, indeed of post-nineteenth century, views of history) that in all three modes of knowledge there must be (if we are to regard them as valid knowing), an element of historical fact which acts as a control. As we learned from our consideration of history in the foregoing chapter, the historian remains in dialogue with his facts and the moment there are no facts to be in dialogue with, we cease to have any 'knowledge' of Jesus at all: we are simply conceptualising a figure of our own conceiving. We have passed from the *datum* of history to the speculations of philosophy.

My point can be put another way. I must be able to have confidence (if I am to accept the christian faith that Jesus was and is God expressed in terms of human personality) that the Christ whom I know 'in faith' is personally continuous with the Jesus of the Gospels and with the Jesus who was born of Mary and grew up in Nazareth. Martin Buber pointed to the distinction between knowing a thing and knowing a person. In fact 'knowing' is fully possible only with regard to persons, since only with persons is there the possibility of entering into an experience of relationship, of having a 'come-back', or having to accommodate one's own self-willing to the self-willing of another. If then I say that I 'know' Christ, I mean, not that I have a philosophical concept which might be labelled 'Christ', but that I am in a personal relationship of out-go and response. The person with whom I am thus in relationship must (if the christian idea of incarnation is to be in any way maintained) be one who possesses the continuous experience of being born of Mary, growing up in Palestine, conducting a ministry, suffering death by crucifixion, re-awakening to life and entering into a new relationship with his Church. The assumptions of Dr Perrin's study, and of the extreme form-critical school would in my opinion destroy all confidence that the necessary degree of personal and historical continuity in 'Jesus Christ' had been preserved. I cannot acquiesce then in the notion that we could lose touch with Jesus as an historical person and still have faith in him religiously.

I do not, however, accept the assumptions of the 'form-critical' school of New Testament scholarships. I come to the reading of the Gospels from the study of the Old Testament, in which study incidentally the 'form-critical' technique was first evolved.[14] The old Testament parallels with the earlier strata of the Gospels are not, in my judgement, Exodus 1–15, or even the Elijah-Elisha cycles in Kings I and II; the closer parallels are with Isaiah 1–12, Amos, Hosea, Micah, Habakkuk, Zephaniah—in other words, those parts of the Old Testament where the legend-making, mythopoeic forces are less in evidence and where the sense of historical fact is strongest. Disciples were accustomed to collect anthologies of their master's sayings: they did it for Isaiah, Amos, Hosea, and in the Q source in the Gospels they did it for Jesus. The fact that the selection of those sayings may well have been largely determined by the needs of the Early Church, and the fact that many of the sayings did serve those needs, and the fact that some small proportion

[14] The form-critical school has in fact relied too exclusively on evidence arrived at by one line of investigation only. Dr Morna Hooker's comment is very apt: 'Valuable as the study of tradition may be, the analysis of individual sayings can sometimes conceal the truth, for the attempt to classify the different strata of tradition can divide the material to such an extent that one can no longer see the whole pattern.' *The Son of Man in Mark*, London and Montreal, 1967, p. 193. The exponents of 'Form-criticism' are also in my opinion too confident of their ability to establish criteria: e.g. 'this idea must be attributed to the Early Church and cannot possibly have been one originating with Jesus.' As a result they have tended to overlook the strong tradition of respect for history, in which the evangelists stood, and in particular have given insufficient weight to Luke's forthright claim to be writing history. He gives every indication of knowing what history is—note his careful preface to his Gospel. His claim is moreover supported by the fact that the rôle of the 'prophets' in Acts and in the Epistles is minimal, whereas that of the apostles as eyewitnesses of the ministry, as well as of the death and resurrection of Jesus is greatly stressed. Cf. Acts 1:21–22.

of gospel sayings are almost certainly the fabrication of the
Early Church, does not alter the major truth that the Gospels
give me a dependable account of Jesus' teaching. Moreover, the
narratives of his actions are for the most part consonant with
the sayings: from Q and Mark and Luke and even Matthew a
recognisably consistent figure emerges. It is he whom I 'know',[15]
and he whom I have now to judge and assess, as honestly as I

[15] I am doing less than justice to Dr Perrin's very able and carefully
argued presentation, but an adequate answer would require a whole book of
equal length of his own, and indeed a range of New Testament scholarship
equal to his own, which I do not possess. For the most part, I have to say
that his arguments leave me unsatisfied, and let it go at that. There is,
however, one point where I should perhaps comment a little further. He
writes on p. 239: 'At this point, we are at the parting of the ways so far as the
discussion of the 'question of the historical Jesus' is concerned. On the right
we have the presupposition that the Incarnation—or the biblical concept of
God active in history or the traditional view of Christianity as related to
certain revelational events in history—that this demands a real and close
relationship between historical knowledge and faith-knowledge, and that
justice must be done to this in our discussion of the question of the historical
Jesus.' To this I warmly assent, though I would have phrased differently
the last clause 'and that justice . . . ' in order to avoid the implication that the
doctrinal requirements might sway our judgement on historical matters. I
would rather say that there must be a tenable view of the close relationship
of historical-knowledge and faith-knowledge to allow any idea of incarnation
to remain viable. Dr Perrin continues: 'On the left we have the conviction
that, even if we may speak meaningfully of God, or the transcendent, none
the less the essential relativity of all historical events means that we cannot
think in terms of a knowledge of Jesus that is different *in kind* from knowledge we may have of other historical persons. So either Jesus becomes an
example of an existential relationship with the transcendent, supreme but
capable of being imitated (Jaspers) or he becomes the 'decisive' manifestation
of that which may also be known elsewhere (Ogden). No doubt other
variations of this theme could be found, but they would all be variations on
the one theme, that faith-knowledge is historic knowledge.' Again, because
of my understanding of the terms 'God' and 'man', I can assent to this, so
long as I am allowed the proviso that if I am a believing christian and know
Jesus in a contemporary, worshipping relationship, my faith-knowledge of
him will also in some ways transcend my 'historic' knowledge; otherwise,
there is an *a priori* assumption hidden in the premises of this view that
there can in fact be no such thing as 'faith-knowledge'. This does not seem
to me to be a possible assumption, since men *do* have a 'historic' knowledge
of Jesus and they *do* have a faith-knowledge of him: that is, they do say
(rightly or mistakenly) of the historical Jesus 'My Lord and my God'; and

can. It is he who challenges me with that penetrating question 'Who say you that I am?'[16]

What then does Jesus teach? His teaching is profoundly simple and significantly profound. To put it down baldly on paper is almost inevitably to make a travesty of it, but nevertheless it has to be attempted. He taught us to call God 'Father'; to think of all men and women as our brothers and sisters; to seek the Kingdom of God; and to recognise in him the personal activity of God in human affairs.

In each of these four statements there is a rich volume of implication and I must at least indicate something of what I have been able to understand from them. To call God 'Father' may arise from nothing more than an unhealthy infantilism— the kind of religious retrogression to the womb of which Freudian psychology has made so much, and which the 'God is dead' theologians are so vigorously combating. But as I read the teaching of Jesus I do not find him encouraging sentimentality and certainly not infantilism. Rather, he seems to me to be saying three things of profound significance—inherited largely from the Hebrew tradition, but re-thought and given the stamp of his own conviction. First, that God is good. The Hebrews knew full well that this was not something to be easily

---

that can never be simply a matter of 'historic' knowledge only. It arises also out of a present relationship. Dr Perrin concludes his paragraph: 'Finally, in the centre, we have Bultmann, whose position may be expressed, in our terms, as maintaining that the three kinds of knowledge are separate and must be kept separate.' It is this third position (which is also Dr Perrin's own view of the matter) which I find particularly unsatisfactory, as virtually denying *ab initio* the validity of the christian concept of incarnation and as losing sight of the necessity for the element of historical fact to exercise its controlling function in the formulation of christian apprehension of Jesus. When we cease to hold on to historical fact, Christianity becomes only a complex of philosophical speculations, and in that respect, at least, a neo-gnosticism; and the inadequacy of gnosticism has many times been demonstrated in the life of the church.

[16] Mark 8:29.

assumed. Life for them was at many times hard and desperate. Jesus and his fellow peasants lived dangerously near the starvation line and food often figures significantly in his thinking. It was a time of wars and civil unrest, when violent death might strike at any moment. It was not easy to say 'Life is good; God is good'. The Book of Ecclesiastes and the Book of Job had both wrestled, in Jesus' own tradition, with this fundamental question—can we believe in the goodness of God?[17] That to answer negatively was a live option in the first christian century is clearly indicated by the constant concern of the popular apocalyptic literature with theodicy, the attempt 'to justify the ways of God to man'. But Jesus chose to reaffirm the conviction of his people that life is good ('God saw everything that he had made and behold it was very good') and that God is good ('O give thanks to the Lord, for he is good'). If at times appearances persuade otherwise, a man must have faith, and endure, believing that in the end all will be set in order, justice will be done, and the goodness of God will be apparent to all: 'he who endures to the end, the same shall be saved'. Here then is Jesus facing one of the really great issues in life, perhaps the greatest. I sometimes think that the really fundamental difference between the religious man, of any faith, and the non-religious lies most characteristically here: the religious man believes in the fundamental goodness of life. Jesus did so believe, with intense conviction and it comes out strongly in his use of this term 'Father'.

In that use he also affirms his belief in the personal nature of the relationship between God and man. 'What man of you, if his son asks him for a loaf, will give him a stone?—how much more will your Father who is in heaven give good things to

[17] The 19th century saw the Book of Job in terms of its own interests: 'Why do men suffer?' But the primary concern of the book is not with the problem of pain but with the problem of the nature of God; can Job really believe in a good and benevolent power in the universe? It is a very modern piece of writing.

those who ask him?' God has a father's knowledge of, and concern for, each one of his children. This again was clearly in the tradition he had inherited ('Lord, thou hast searched me and known me') but Jesus endows this thought with a new quality of insight into the fatherly concern of God for the individual. This is well illustrated by his story which usually goes under the title of 'the Prodigal Son', but which would more appropriately be called 'the Forgiving Father'. In the tale, the father sweeps every other consideration aside as second to this: 'he was dead to us and is alive again, he was lost to us and is found'. We may have real intellectual difficulties in accepting the teaching of Jesus at this point, and be honestly hesitant to believe that God can simultaneously have a personal interest in and concern for each individual now alive on this teeming planet of ours, but that this was a central conviction in the mind of Jesus does not allow of a moment's doubt. By his use of this term 'Father', Jesus taught the direct, personal concern of the Divine Power in the universe for each and every one of us: 'if God so clothes the grass of the field . . . will he not much more clothe you, O men of little faith?'

Even so, in his use of this term 'Father', Jesus is not giving the slightest encouragement to infantilism. That is something we too often have imported into his teaching. On the contrary he challenges men to exercise a healthy maturity in this relationship. When for example, he is urging that men should be adult and wise in their own relationships, not being given to petty retaliations and revenges, he reminds them that to live in this way is to be true sons of their Father. To be a true son is to be like your father, and to respond to situations with a like response to his in a similar situation. So to be adult and mature in human relationships is to be like God, for that is how he is with us: 'Love your enemies, pray for those who persecute you, so that you may be sons of your Father who is in heaven, for he makes his sun to rise on the evil and on the good, and sends rain on the just and the unjust'. There is nothing immature or unhealthily dependent in the relationship of man with God when it makes such challenging demands upon him: 'you therefore shall be perfect, as your heavenly Father is perfect'. Nor, we may add, is there anything sentimental in a relationship which can allow for God asking of his son that he endure death by crucifixion to further the divine purposes of good for all mankind. In his exposition by word and example of this central concept in all his thinking, Jesus offers me the ideal of a fully adult, truly mature relationship of God and man. On Jesus' lips the term 'Father' is not one to be used lightly, but arises out of deep conviction.[18]

Jesus teaches that because God is their Father all men are brothers. Basically this means recognising the inherent rights of the personal mode of being. I am a person and demand existentially to be treated as a person; to love another is to recognise his equal right to be treated fully as a person. Reinhold Niebuhr has reminded us that in all life, benevolence is not enough; we need political programmes and economic theories and social moralities; similarly in individual lives we need counsellors and physicians and psychiatrists to inform and correct our relationships; but as the world-wide failure of marxism has demonstrated, a political-economic theory is not sufficient for the structuring of the life of either societies or individuals—a deep concern for persons as persons is also absolutely necessary. To forget this is to suppress individuality and freedom, and these will not be suppressed. Poets will write poetry, and artists will paint pictures, and *Dr Zhivago* will insist on being written. The strife for civil rights, the world-wide protest against colonialism, the folk-movement revolt against war, even the negative protest of the 'beatniks' who have 'given up' on society, all stem from this common root: the

[18] Cf. the sensitive work by W. F. Lofthouse, *The Father and the Son, A Study in Johannine Thought*, London, 1934.

existential need to be recognised and treated as persons. All these phenomena are the adolescent signs of man's coming of age: he is asking to be treated as a fully mature and adult person. These phenomena are in fact an assertion of our need that we should love one another; and for Jesus this is natural and proper, since God is our Father and all men are brothers. In contrast to the Greeks, in contrast to the Buddha, Jesus placed a personal concern and a sense of social responsibility in the very foremost place in his hierarchy of values. You should seek to love your neighbour as yourself, he taught; and who is your neighbour? Anyone who is in need. If you are, he said, approaching the altar itself to make an offering to God on high, and you remember that you are at odds with your brother, first go and seek reconciliation with him and then return and worship. When you pray, ask God to be reconciled to you in so far as and because you have extended reconciliation to your fellows: 'forgive us our trespasses, as we forgive those that trespass against us'. This is the touchstone, this is the decisive criterion, this is the highest and foremost in all the hierarchy of a man's many personal and social concerns.

I have to interrupt my exposition of the teaching of Jesus to make this comment. In this teaching of the primacy of love, I find a practical wisdom, a deep insight into the nature of man and into the true character of social relationships, such as puts Jesus in a class apart from all other teachers. No one else that I know has the same penetrating simplicity, the same assured understanding of the needs of the individual and of society. The priority which Jesus accords to personal values enables us to use all the abilities of economics and sociology and the human sciences to truly significant effect, but without this first and most basic of all understandings, our social endeavours and our personal services become distorted, twisted, and end as a caricature of what they set out to become. Neither socialism nor the social sciences are enough; this I have learned for

myself; but I have to go back to the teaching of Jesus time and
time again to be renewed in an understanding of why they are
not enough: unless they are motivated through and through
by love they fall prey to perversion. As that great interpreter
of the mind of Jesus put it: 'if I give all my goods to feed the
poor, if I give my body to be burned (one might almost think
that Paul had foreseen the tragedy of Viet-nam) if I have
not love, I have accomplished nothing.' But it must be a
perceptive, mature love, a true recognition of the inherent
right of the other person to be treated as a person: 'do to
others as you need them to do to you.' This is an area of life
where I can put the teaching of Jesus to the crucial test and
when I have done so I have to recognise that I am convinced
by him as by no other teacher in all the history of mankind. He is contemporary: he speaks to my society and my
condition.

One of the enigmas of the New Testament is that the most
common phrase on the lips of Jesus 'the Kingdom of God',
had dropped out of the vocabulary of his followers by the time
the second generation of christians produced its written
records, that is, The Acts, the Pauline corpus and the Johannine writings. This incidentally is a contributory reason for
thinking that the Synoptic Gospels do convey a basically true
impression of the historic Jesus and of his teaching: Jesus as
depicted in the Gospels is not assimilated to the speech-
patterns of the Early Church. But the phenomenon nevertheless
has to be explained. I find the clue in the history of the concept. The Old Testament presents its story on the one side as
a quest, and on the other as a promise; it begins with Abraham
seeking a land and God promising to give that land to him.
Abraham finds his land and the promise that he would settle
in it is fulfilled, and yet not wholly: he is only a 'resident alien'
whereas he wants it for his own, and for his family and clan,
so that they may become a people, having an identity, 'a pride

of ancestry and a hope of posterity'. The descent into Egypt is a regression from the hope which only heightens its longing; under Moses the promised land is sought anew, but now the movement acquires the character of a folk-emigration from slavery and oppression, and a folk-immigration into freedom and dignity. But the reality is only a tenuous and precarious existence on the least desirable areas of Palestine, the bare hills and the semi-arid seasonal pasturages. There is little unity among the scattered Hebrew groups, and little hope for the future, until suddenly David arrives on the scene and transforms the whole situation. The Hebrews are united, given the whole land, given access to sources of wealth, given a capital, given a national shrine, given a hegemony among the peoples of Palestine. The promise to Abraham has been fulfilled and the quest of Israel has reached its goal; David's generation of Hebrews were literally living in 'the Kingdom of God' with its capital at Jerusalem.

But then the vision fades and again the reality is found to be less than glorious. David's Kingdom falls apart, and the political weakness of the divided kingdoms set men longing for a better state of society, and not for Israel only but for other people also—in some passages the ideal world is seen as the result of conquest, but in others it is attained by reason of conviction and the spread of understanding. So the prophetic concept of 'the Day of Yahweh' is born, and men nurse the eschatological hope of the day of divine intervention, the ushering in of the Golden Age. When the prophetic movement fails it is succeeded by the apocalyptic movement, and the comparatively staid prophetic expectation is translated into the bizarre visions of Daniel and the Enoch literature. But there were also others who entertained a more spiritual, more individual hope, such as nourished the piety of the group out of which emerged the anthology we call the Book of Psalms; their longing expresses itself in the older phraseology:

Yet a little while, and the wicked will be no more;
though you look well at his place, he will not be there.
But the meek shall possess the land,
and delight themselves in abundant prosperity.[19]

Here 'possess the land' has obviously become the symbol for a much wider, deeper aspiration: to enter into all the fulness of the promise of God, a promise which, as it is attained, is forever changing its nature and leading men on to a vision of something new, something more wonderful, something infinitely more desirable. So, too, Jesus reverts to the old, poetic language when he says: 'Blessed are the meek for they shall "inherit the land".' By translating this as 'inherit the earth' we have given this saying a quite erroneous meaning—that the meek will come to positions of power and influence in the world. But Jesus meant that 'the meek' (the deeply-religious, non-activist peasantry of his day, such as are portrayed in the opening chapters of Luke's Gospel) would enter into the spiritual promises of God, first disclosed to Abraham and progressively revealed in succeeding generations. His own favourite phrase for this goal of Israel's quest (looking at it from the one side) or this inner secret of God's unfolding promise (looking at it from the other side) was 'the Kingdom of God', a phrase which had become popular in Palestine in the inter-testamental period. It did not translate well into Hellenistic-Roman thought; it had too much of a political flavour and the early church dropped it in favour of the term 'salvation', thereby giving the ancient hope a new twist, an overly-individual, an overly-psychological connotation. For Jesus, however, 'the Kingdom of God' was a phrase indicating for the individual a rightness of attitude to God and a rightness of attitude to one's fellow men and women, translated into such

19 Psalm 37:10–11.

practicalities of life that a community, 'the true Israel', must inevitably result.

The Kingdom, then, is for Jesus an orientation of heart and mind towards God and man, giving rise to a renewed community. The individual acceptance of, or entrance into, the Kingdom is possible now; its emergence within the small community of his disciples is proleptic of the rehabilitated and purified society which would emerge when a majority of men and women had accepted the Kingdom into their hearts. The Kingdom is for the individual who discovers it the pearl of great price, the treasure hidden in the field; the Kingdom in society is the leaven working in the mass, it is the grain of mustard seed growing up to become a great bush. The Kingdom of God is within us and among us, and we pray every day 'Thy Kingdom come'. To be a follower of Jesus is to accept the Kingdom as a personal discipline and way of life, as a pattern of relationships and as a goal of hope for one's self and for the human race.

The other enigma of the Gospel story is the occurrence of the phrase 'the Son of Man'. Again, according to our records, it is a phrase constantly on the lips of Jesus, and again it is strangely and conspicuously absent from the conversation, preaching and writing of the second wave of christians, the people who produced the New Testament. There are three possibilities: that the Synoptic record reflects more or less faithfully the usage of Jesus, or that Jesus used the phrase but his usage of it has been badly misinterpreted, or that he did not use the phrase but it has been foisted on to him by his apocalyptically-minded followers. The scholarly debate has been long and warmly contested.[20] For myself, I judge that

[20] To name only recent works in English, one can point to N. Perrin, *op. cit.* pp. 164–206; A. J. B. Higgins, *Jesus and the Son of Man*, London, 1964; M. D. Hooker, *The Son of Man in Mark*, London and Montreal, 1967. Norman Perrin denies that Jesus used the phrase at all; A. J. B. Higgins allows that Jesus used the phrase, but not of himself in his present existence—

Jesus did use the phrase; that it derived from his Galilean background of folk-apocalyptic; that it puzzled his followers not familiar with that background (that is, the second-wave, often Hellenistic, christians) and was often misinterpreted in their reporting; that it speedily fell out of use, because of translation difficulties and uncertainty as to meaning; and that it gave way all the more quickly because two other phrases were much more readily meaningful, 'Messiah' and 'Son of God'. Whether Jesus used the phrase of himself alone, or of himself and his community as 'the saints of God' is not wholly clear, but the obviously communal aspect of the figure in Daniel 7 (from which 'the son of man' figure in apocalyptic derives) suggests probably an ambivalent usage, sometimes 'I' and sometimes 'we'.[21] The important thing about the phrase is to recall that it contains no element of self-depreciation (lowly 'son of man' over against glorious 'Son of God') but rather, in accordance with its origin in Daniel, it claims for the person or community thus designated a central, indeed culminating rôle in the outworking of God's plan in history; the 'Son of Man' is God's participant, even God's Agent, in bringing history to its triumphant conclusion.

---

he may have identified himself with the Son of Man in a future existence, i.e. he expected to become the Son of Man at the time of eschatological judgement. Morna Hooker's view is that Jesus used the phrase of himself 'to claim authority, accept the necessity for suffering, and confidently affirm ultimate vindication' (*op. cit.* p. 191). Dr Hooker also points out that the phrase has meaning in the situation of Jesus, but none in the situation of the Early Church. Since the latter believed Jesus to be risen, vindicated and ascended, titles like 'Christ', 'Lord', 'Son of God', had become appropriate. Hence the occurrence of the phrase in the records of the ministry of Jesus and its disappearance from later strata of christian sources. (*op. cit.* p. 189f.). This seems to me very cogent reasoning. Dr Hooker, a former student of mine, is now Lecturer in New Testament at King's College, London. Cf. also the significant support given for this assessment by Professor C. K. Barrett of Durham University, in his recent book *Jesus and the Gospel Tradition*, London, 1967, especially p. 33.

[21] This oscillation between an individual and corporate reference is very familiar to anyone who has studied the use of 'I' in the Psalms.

In other words, if Jesus used this phrase at all, it must have been to assert a particular significance for his own rôle in history. The older and more familiar concept of Messiah would have done this more easily (and at this stage the title 'Son of God' was part of the messianic tradition rather than an independent concept) but Jesus was probably precluded from using it on two grounds: he did not possess sufficiently clearly the necessary physical qualification of being of Davidic descent[22] (this was taken care of in the later nativity legends) and he did not relish the term's strong nationalist-political associations. Away from Palestine, in an international movement the political implications could be more satisfactorily explained away ('my kingdom is not of this world', says Jesus to Pilate in the Johannine account of their interview) and so 'Messiah' or Greek 'Christ' became the favourite designation of Jesus for the second-wave christians. It also gave access to the 'Son of God' phrase, and this was congenial to early theologisers also. But Jesus himself, it would seem, found the phrase 'Son of Man' more meaningful and more pliable; it could more easily be shaped to his own ideas. So he used the term 'Son of Man', but his followers used the term 'Christ'.

The important point in this discussion of titles, however, is that by it we are having our attention drawn to what is the most striking fact about the teaching of Jesus: his assertion of himself as personally significant in the outworking of God's process in history. Jesus, (even whether or not he used the title Son of Man and whether or not he claimed to be the Messiah) arrogates to himself an importance and an authority which is not claimed by any other teacher, ancient or modern. All others point away from themselves to something other: Moses to the Torah, the Buddha to enlightenment, Confucius to the Law of Order, Muhammad to the revelation of God's will—but

[22] Mark 12:35 f. is extremely significant, in that Jesus challenges in this saying the importance of Davidic descent for the Messiah figure.

Jesus says 'Come, follow me'. He says: 'Who ever would save his life will lose it, and whoever loses his life for my sake and the gospel's will save it'; and again, 'who ever is ashamed of me and of my words in this adulterous and sinful generation, of him will the Son of man also be ashamed when he comes in the glory of the Father and of the holy angels'; 'come to me, all who labour and are heavy-laden, and I will give you rest'. There may be indeed in the present form of these and comparable sayings in all strata of the Gospel records, re-touchings which are the work of the Early Church; but Jesus' sense of personal destiny, his assertion that he personally is the challenging fact in the experience of mankind, this surely goes back to Jesus himself. The question he put to his immediate followers he therefore puts to us with equal insistence: 'Who do you say I am?'[23] It is a judgement we cannot, having once met with him, avoid.

It is this which for me brings to the focus of decision the whole enquiry of this study. I began from the existential situation: a being located in an ecology of physical, chemical, biological processes, knowing myself to be the product of evolution and recognising that I am but a small fleck of foam on the hurrying stream of history, but even so a person having self-awareness and a measure of free-will. I also know that as a person I have a right to be treated as a person, a right to expect a personal response from the universe which has produced me; I believe that that response does in fact make itself known to me, and I call it 'God'. I am then a theistic believer. But I know further that the christian tradition asserts of Jesus of Nazareth that he is God expressed in terms of human personality; I have sought a way in which I can accommodate that thought of incarnation to the insights of my generation, and to the nature of personality as I understand it;

[23] Mark 8: 27–30.

I then scrutinise the teaching of Jesus and I find it to be perceptive and in terms of values convincing. The theistic faith
I find to be rationally established, but the christian faith is
contingent: it *could* all be true, but *is* it? My answer to that
question depends on the answer I make to this prior question,
which Jesus himself put to his disciples: 'Who do you think I
am?'

I am not disturbed by the fact that everything turns on a
personal judgement of an historical event, mediated to us
through the uncertainties of scholarly research. Lessing, on the
basis of his acceptance of the views of Reimarus with regard to
the life of Jesus, put forward his famous proposition: *Zufällige
Geschichtswahrheiten können der Beweis von notwendigen Ver-
nunftswahrheiten nie werden;* 'the accidental truth of history can
never become the necessary proofs of reason'. On this Dr
Perrin comments 'With *Glaube* (faith) substituted for *Vernunft*
(reason) this is a view-point widely accepted in our current
discussion'.[24] There is, however, a whole world of difference
between Lessing's original saying (with which surely everyone
must agree: 'from is to ought, there is no way which logic has
not blocked') and Dr Perrin's new version. Reason is sustained
by intellectual argument, not by historical event; but faith
while it should never be unreasonable goes beyond reasoning.
Faith is an activity, it is living in a certain way, it is making
certain existential choices, it is choosing to be this and refusing
to be that. Faith therefore requires more than an argument to
create it and sustain it. In fact, I never have faith in any argument; I only have faith in a person. Only a person can justify
faith, and a person is a phenomenon in space and time, an
event in history. Thus I am prepared to stake everything on
the answer to a question in history, for in fact I have no other
choice. Either I accept the historical Jesus as Master and Lord,

[24] *Op. cit.* pp. 210–211.

or I reject him. It is as simple as that. Jesus himself has seen to it that there can be no middle way.[25]

The answer I make can, in the nature of things, be only a personal one. I have to say that while I am no fabulous scholar, I have read fairly widely and I have certainly travelled far, and I have thought on these matters to the best of my ability. I am more than cursorily acquainted with non-christian teachings and with other cultures than my own. I am fairly familiar with Judaism, in its many ranges and varieties, and believe I can understand something of the emotional grasp which jewishness has upon a jew. I have been intimate with muslims, and sharing something of their faith, I have counted it a privilege, in Kenneth Cragg's expressive phrase, to leave my sandals at the door of the mosque. I have responded in my reading to the urbanity and gentle sanity of the traditional Chinese teaching; I have thrilled to Plato and I have revelled in the brilliance that was Greece; I have studied rewardingly the wealth of philosophical and religious thought that has emanated from India, and for Gautama Buddha I have the very deepest and most profound respect; but I have also to say that none of these challenges me as does Jesus of Nazareth. This is not, I believe, the result of mere traditionalism—that I have been brought up to revere him, and to think of him as in a class apart; I have lived for a number of years among hard-headed and very sceptical non-believers, and I have myself cultivated an honest and enquiring spirit, and I have sought never to avoid the implications of anything that I had to accept as true. The fact remains that I am not aware that any other teacher or person makes such demands upon me as does Jesus of Nazareth. By

[25] Cf. the 'either—or' character of the claims he made upon his disciples' loyalty; for example, Luke 9: 57–62. I would agree with Dr Perrin (see note 15 above) that our knowledge of the 'historical' Jesus is also 'historic knowledge, and that once our choice is made it passes on into 'faith-knowledge'; but even so the crucial choice has to be made at the level of our historical knowledge of Jesus of Nazareth.

his teaching of 'the Kingdom', he challenges me to be every day more of a person. Being a person is the most important fact of my existence and it is just here that Jesus impresses me most deeply: he is himself so much of a person. To accept his view of life, to share (insofar as I am able) his faith in God, to try to adopt in daily living his attitude to my fellow men and women, in the home, in the office, in administrative relationships, in social moralities, in political judgements, in intellectual assessments, and then further to attempt the consonant self-discipline and nurture of my individuality—this demands of me that I should constantly be achieving a new maturity, a deeper understanding of life, a new capacity for love. Jesus requires of me in fact to be more of a person than I really am, and he does so with an authority to which I can only respond by calling him Master and Lord. I thereby accept his estimate of God as Father, and of himself as Son of Man; I seek to recognise all men as my brothers, I pray for the coming of God's Kingdom, and I seek to live by its standards and ideals. I am a christian.

It is still true, however, even here, in the moment of decision that I have to remember that I think in myths, that terms like 'Father' and 'Son of Man' or 'the expression of God in terms of human personality' are only models of reality. These phrases are metaphorical rather than ontological; I talk in parables because (like Jesus) without a parable I cannot speak, not even to myself. But knowing that my language is not absolute is part of my faith in Jesus: I trust him that when I say God is Father, and that he is Son of Man and God's Messiah, I am not very far from the truth. These are beliefs, my linguistic 'models' which I may have to adapt and change, but I have confidence that as I continue to explore my existential situation my faith in God and in Jesus will prove to have been rightly placed. Therefore, taking the Creed as a religious whole rather than as an analysable complex, I can meaningfully recite 'I believe in God, the Father Almighty, and in Jesus Christ, the only-begotten Son of God, begotten of his Father before all words, God of God, light of light, being of one substance with the Father, by whom all things were made'; thus it is also that at Christmas time I can joyfully enter again into the old legends, and share anew the Christ-child myth, and sing once more of the mystery of the incarnation:

> *Our God contracted to a span,*
> *Incomprehensibly made man.*

For I have faith in Jesus. I do believe that in him God expressed himself in terms of human personality and shared our human existence with us. *Ergo Christianus sum.* Thus I am a christian.

Chapter Seven

HIS DEATH AND RESURRECTION

IF Christmas Day is the most religious day of the year, then Good Friday is the most christian. By this I mean that the idea of God being made known, and being made available to us mortal men, is the very stuff of religion. The religious interpretation of life conceives both the reality and the accessibility of divine power—it is here and we can lay hold on it. It is to this conviction that in their varying ways all religions testify, and in the West, it is this thought which Christmas Day celebrates. But the distinctively christian thought is that man is alienated from God by moral fault, and that the death of Jesus has restored man to the relationship he ought to have with God. Good Friday is the day when this teaching is particularly set forth, but throughout the year the idea is architectonic for the whole of christian thought and practice.

> *He died that we might be forgiven,*
> *He died to make us good,*
> *That we might go at last to heaven,*
> *Saved by his precious blood.*

In that simple children's hymn is a summary of the christian faith. As the cross is the most distinctive symbol of Christianity and as Holy Communion is the most distinctive act of worship so the doctrine of the atonement is the most distinctive teaching. All the world shares Christmas Day with the Church—they have almost taken it over—but on Good Friday the christian worships alone. It is the most christian day of the year.

If then, as one trying to come to terms with his situation and his tradition, I am convinced of the rightness of the religious rather than the secular interpretation of life, and if I have accepted Jesus of Nazareth as the expression in terms of human personality of the divine power which animates the universe, then I have to face the fact that this christian tradition says that the most important thing he did was to die.[1] The earliest summary of the faith, the Apostles' Creed, begins: 'I believe in God the Father Almighty, Maker of heaven and earth; and in Jesus Christ his only Son our Lord, who was conceived by the Holy Ghost, born of the Virgin Mary, suffered under Pontius Pilate, was crucified, dead and buried'. As has so often been remarked, there is here nothing about his ministry or his teaching—the significant facts are his birth and his death.

Just because this is the core-belief of the christian Church, it is here that devotion and piety are most deeply stirred, it is here that the visual arts, poetry and liturgy, have created their finest offerings, and it is here that religious susceptibilities are most sensitive. Anyone approaching the cross of Jesus needs to heed the injunction to Moses at the burning bush: 'Take off thy shoes from off thy feet, for the ground whereon thou standest is holy ground'. When I visited Palestine, the

---

[1] But not merely to die—rather 'to-die-and-live-again'. Good Friday in christian thought is always followed by Easter Day and there is a grave error from the properly christian point of view in isolating the dying of Jesus as 'the most important thing he did'. But it is a mistake which histori-cally the Church has tended to make, and therefore the dying of Jesus must be discussed separately, and indeed it has its own very distinctive soterio-logical interest.

only site to stir my religious sensitivity (as distinct from my scholarly interests) was the bare rock outcropping amid the ancient olive-trees on the Mount of Olives. Some of those trees are over two thousand years old. The rock was certainly there in Jesus' day. It was on this hillside, it may well have been under those trees, at that rock, that Jesus prayed earnestly, 'Father, let this cup pass from me'. It was here that he chose not to run away but to accept willingly a horrible death. Why? It is a question to which I have to find an answer, and find it reverently.

Jesus stood in the tradition of Israel. He saw his own rôle in terms of that tradition, and it was this tradition which motivated him to accept that death. The Old Testament formulation of the history and significance of Israel had long since taken shape, and this interpretation of what Israel was, and what was her destiny, was presented to Jesus constantly in the life of the synagogue. It is important to remember that he was the child of the synagogue, where lay-leadership in bible study and prayer were characteristic, and not of the Temple where a professional clergy and a cult of sacrificial rites predominated. This fact is demonstrated throughout all his teaching, in his personal relationships and in his attitude to the Temple itself: for him 'the Temple' was not the inner sacerdotal shrine, but the outer courts which provided a forum for free-lance teachers and preachers, as well as a place of prayer for groups and individuals. Ritual sacrifice had, as far as we know, little or no place in his thinking. Rather, his thought centred upon Israel as the nation chosen to be God's people, the recipients of his revelation and the heirs of the promise. The promise was first made to Abraham, and thereafter constantly renewed that the Israelites would inherit 'the land'. 'The land', as I have suggested, was a concept which changed successively over the years but nevertheless preserved an identity of ideal, so that Jesus' own teaching of 'the Kingdom' was in the direct line of evolu-

tion from the patriarchal longing for 'a place of one's own'.
For him, however, 'the Kingdom' had become a way of life.
To be in 'the Kingdom' was to live in this world, in these
circumstances, under the challenge of one's own contingent
existence, yet in a right relationship with God, a right relationship with other men, with an informed knowledge of right and
wrong, and a simple, uncomplicated readiness at all times to
choose that which is right. This way of life implies a corporate
aspect in that the association together of those who have
entered 'the Kingdom' gives rise to a new kind of human society, which is in fact ideal Israel, Israel as it truly ought to be.
When public institutions and sociological structures incorporate
this way of life 'the Kingdom' will have come 'on earth'. So
the Kingdom is already available for the individual and is yet
to come for mankind as a whole.

This was the message which Jesus taught and exemplified. He
believed that in so doing he was taking up and fulfilling the rôle
of Israel. When it became apparent that his mission would meet
with opposition and resentment, he nevertheless persisted.
When the vested interests and the social elements to which
the Kingdom's way of life was a challenge, gave clear indications
of their ruthlessness and their determination to destroy any
opposition (the execution of his predecessor John the Baptist
was such an indication) he nevertheless continued in his mission.
At what he thought was the strategic moment he appealed to
the people over the heads of the established authorities of his
day—politically, the Romans; religiously, the priesthood—and
in response those authorities combined forces to get rid of him.
Whether Jesus ever thought that the form of his death was
likely to be Roman crucifixion we do not know. What is clear
is that when, by riding into Jerusalem on Palm Sunday, he
offered himself to the Jewish people as the embodiment of their
national hopes and the answer to their religious aspirations, he
was prepared for that appeal to fail, and he expected the

authorities to react strongly and decisively. Nevertheless, he was convinced that he had to stand by his vision of the Kingdom. even to the point of dying for it. He further believed that because the Kingdom was revealed through him, his death, if it should take place, would make that Kingdom plain to all men. He expected God to intervene and vindicate him, if not before, then certainly after his death.[2] But he was prepared if necessary to go to death and beyond.[3] This then is what the death of Jesus means to me: a preparedness to surrender life itself, rather than to surrender the vision of what is ultimately good. This death,

[2] The theme of the suffering of Israel, her salvation and vindication is one of the great Old Testament themes—e.g. Exodus 1–15, Ezekiel 37, Isaiah 40–55. The vindication of the individual is indicated by the story of the ascent of Elijah, by the piety of such Psalms as 22, 40, and 116, and by Daniel 12:1–3. Vindication was an idea current from at least the times of the Maccabean martyrs and widespread in Jesus' own day. Whether 'the Servant' complex of ideas in the Deutero-Isaian anthology was particularly influential in the thought of Jesus, is highly doubtful: see Morna Hooker's *Jesus and the Servant*, London, 1959. But Professor Barrett has pointed out that the idea of suffering and vindication is integral to the Son of Man complex, which was in his view central in Jesus' thinking. (*Jesus and the Gospel Tradition*, London, 1967, p. 45). The prophecies in the Gospels (e.g. Mark 8:31) that Jesus would rise from the dead on the third day are to be interpreted therefore as later and much more specific formulations of Jesus' affirmations, in his conversations with the disciples, of his assurance of final vindication.

[3] Professor Barrett has very ably shown the difficulties of arriving at a confident account of Jesus' thoughts and expectations—it is, he says, a particular and central instance of the problem of 'the historical Jesus'. But in his own scholarly and careful way he demonstrates that we can arrive at a tenable position on the main points: that Jesus recognised the possibility of his death, that he interpreted it in accordance with the Son of Man complex of ideas, and that the interpretation included the idea of eventual vindication. Dr Barrett is of the opinion that Jesus hoped for vindication before death, and so died disappointed of that hope. 'It was because (God) was the sort of God Jesus declared him to be ... that Jesus foresaw obedient suffering, followed by vindication, as his own task in the rôle of making God known, and in renewing man's relation with his Creator ... It turned out that the suffering was more acute than the human Jesus had foreseen ... And the vindication was extended and deepened in a way beyond the human imagination of Jesus ... But the very fact that Jesus' human estimates fell so far short of the facts did more to prove him right in principle ... By being mistaken in detail, Jesus was more effectively shown to be right in all that really mattered than he could have been by small-scale accuracy.' *Jesus and the Gospel Tradition*, London, 1967, p. 108.

whenever I contemplate it, evokes my profoundest admiration. It provokes in me a strong desire to emulate him, and to enter the Kingdom myself to share it with him and his. His death is thus indeed redemptive, re-creative for me, in my own human, existential situation.

The first christians were so sure that the dying of Jesus on the cross was of immense significance, indeed of central and ultimate significance, that they cast around for categories in which to present that significance to others. Coming as they did from a Jewish background, it was inevitable that they should employ the category of sacrifice: as (according to the rationale of the Temple cultus) the blood of an animal offered in the proper manner 'dealt with' the sin of the worshipper, so the blood of Jesus, shed when he died according to God's will, 'dealt with'[4] the sin of all mankind. It was a superior sacrifice, in that whereas animal sacrifice was efficacious only for the one who offered it, and even so had constantly to be repeated, the self-sacrifice of Jesus needed only to be offered once and was efficacious for all. Such was the thinking of some of the early interpreters of the death of Jesus, and these ideas have persisted down through the centuries, particularly as the rationale for 'the sacrifice of the Mass'. Later believers, building on one of his own metaphors,[5] interpreted the dying of Jesus as a ransom paid to the Devil, whereby the souls of men, captive to Satan by reason of sin, were released for ever from his power. Anselm in the eleventh century, in one of the great books of all time, *Cur Deus Homo*, introduced the idea that Jesus' death was a payment made to God—his honour had been affronted and 'satisfaction' (in the mediaeval, chivalric sense) was due to him. Man could not render this 'satisfaction' him-

---

[4] The Hebrew term *kipper* is best translated by this vague phrase 'to deal with' because, whatever its etymology, this is what it had come to mean in religious practice. The usual 'to make atonement for' mistranslates and reprehensibly over-translates.

[5] Mark 10:45.

self, so God had sent his son into the lists in man's place. In the seventeenth and eighteenth centuries this thinking was elaborated into theories of 'vicarious punishment': satisfaction (now in a legal sense) must be exacted, but in mercy God laid the penalty on his Son, who died in man's stead. Despite their close connection with, if not origination from, the eminent international lawyer Grotius, a great many of these later ideas are an affront to legal and moral thought alike, but they were nevertheless the categories in which christians, particularly the products of the successive Evangelical Revivals of the eighteenth and nineteenth centuries, expressed their convictions relating to the dying of Jesus.

These, and other similar interpretations of the dying of Jesus are described by the theologians as 'objective' theories of the Atonement. They teach that when Jesus died on the cross, something happened which affected profoundly the relationship of all mankind with God, quite apart from any individual reaction to it. But at least as far back as Abelard in the twelfth century, some christians have recognised that the death of Jesus is important because of the impact it has upon those who contemplate it:

> *When I survey the wondrous cross,*
> *Where the young Prince of Glory died,*
> *My richest gain I count but loss,*
> *And pour contempt on all my pride.*

This kind of thinking has not been popular with theologians. It is described in contrast to the 'objective' theories as 'subjective', and deemed to be shallow and inadequate. Abelard has never been raised to the dignity of sainthood! It seems to me, however, that those who try to maintain the superior value of an 'objective' theory of the Atonement are really trying to retain an impersonal and therefore in the last analysis a superstitious view of religion. The idea that something happened two thousand years ago, to which I can in this day have recourse, so that my selfishness of yesterday and my foolish decision of a year ago, and my life-long lack of single-mindedness and nobility of purpose, are somehow or other 'dealt with', and I am no longer personally responsible or accountable for these things (i.e. the guilt attaching to these things has been done away, 'forgiven') arises from a childish longing for a talismanic cure-all. Blood, even Jesus' blood, can do nothing about last week's bout of bad temper and all its unfortunate consequences. God is not proud that his honour should demand 'satisfaction', nor is he immoral that he should be other than nauseated by the notion of 'vicarious punishment'. The phrase 'moral influence theory', which as related to the atonement has been all too often used in a perjurative sense, nevertheless indicates the only kind of approach which can today be considered as mature. The interpretation of the dying of Jesus as a redemptive event is consonant with twentieth century ideas of morality and personal responsibility only if it is effective in the sphere of ideas, that is, of influential concepts. The christian should meditate after this manner: 'Jesus was a man prepared to die for his vision of the truth: he is an example which shames and inspires other men to rise above their mediocre selves to a finer quality of living—the quality of the Kingdom itself. He lived and died for the Kingdom; as his follower, I also must live by the Kingdom, and, if necessary, die for it. From this realisation I draw a renewal of resolve, a whole new direction of life, whereby I become indeed "a new man in Christ"'. Such a meditation reminds us that not a process, and certainly not a transaction, but only a person can be redemptive in the personal realm.

It may be said—it will be said—that I have not taken into account the depths of iniquity in the human heart. According to classic christian theology, a burden of guilt lies upon the conscience, which only the cross of Christ can take away. But this needs closer inspection. It implies an outmoded thought-form of God, as Judge or King. God is not a judge before whom we stand as guilty offenders against divine law; nor is he a king, whose feudal seigneurial rights we have invaded; these are myths, which have in times past served more or less adequately to express the divine-human relationship, but now do so no longer. Rather, we know God as Creator, and ourselves as the products of his creativity, struggling out of our evolutionary past into our as yet unknown but ever imperious future. We are not responsible for that past, but we are responsible for that future. We must live conscious of that future, and we must live individually and collectively for that future.

It is very important in the discussion of these matters, perhaps even more important than at any other point in this whole reappraisal of the christian religion, to make sure that our religious thinking is consonant with the rest of our concepts and ideas. It is essential that we recognise that ideas cannot long remain convincing theologically once they have become obsolete sociologically. The notion, for example, that crime merits punishment has long since died in enlightened educational and penological thought and is fast being left behind in society in general. Penologists now recognise that penalties can only be justified in terms of their deterrent or rehabilitatory character, a point which is well made by the following exchange, which took place on a British radio programme: 'Robin Day: . . . "And in particular, what emphasis should be placed on punishment—on the simple principle which a good many people believe in, that wickedness deserves punishment—and that for wrong-doing there must be retribution?" Lady Wooton: "I should put the punishment of wickedness at the bottom of my list of objectives. I don't like the word 'punishment'; I have great difficulty in using it. I think you have sometimes to make things unpleasant for offenders, but if you are going to try and measure wickedness, you have to get inside another man's skin. You don't know what the temptation was, you don't know how much his character has been formed by the world in which he lived, the kind of family he came from. And I think there is another reason why one should not pay too much attention to wickedness; weakmindedness and mental disorder get more and more blurred, so that we cannot define wickedness as we used to. And on top of that the wicked are not necessarily the people who do the most damage." Robin Day: "You would then discard punishment altogether from any set of aims in passing sentence?". Lady Wooton: "If by punishment you mean something which is related to the personal wickedness of the offender.'"[6]

It is ideas such as these which are motivating the administration of justice in progressive countries, and it is with ideas such as these that our thinking about man's sin and God's reaction to it must be of one piece. If God is God in any sense worthy of the term, he knows all about our past; he understands it much better than we do, and in that sense he 'forgives' us all that we have ever done or said or been. That is a great and

---

[6] Cf. *The Listener*, August 18, 1966, p. 225. Barbara Wooton, who was herself a Justice of the Peace for sixteen years, was formerly Professor of Social Studies, London University, and is the author of, among other works, *Social Science and Social Pathology*, London, 1959. (Cf. especially the chapter 'Mental Disorder and the Problem of Moral and Criminal Responsibility', pp. 227–267). If it be rejoined that the difference between God and Lady Wooton is that he does know just what she does not, we have to recall Voltaire's epigram: 'Tout savoir c'est tout pardonner'. It may also not be inappropriate to quote the tombstone quatrain from 17th century Chichester:

> Here lies Martin Elginbrodde,
> Have mercy on my soul, Lord God.
> As I would have, an I were God,
> And thou wert Martin Elginbrodde.

Every man who is honest with himself acknowledges his faults, but he also believes he deserves not divine wrath but divine mercy. He knows he is more sinned against than sinning. This recognition has certainly changed penological views on crime and punishment, but at the same time has made 'objective' views of the atonement anachronistic in the second half of the twentieth century.

blessed truth—but it did not need the death of Jesus to tell us of it. A thoughtful muslim can be equally as assured of God's forgiveness as can a christian. As for particular crimes, of cruelty or greed or arrogance or lust, we have to learn to disapprove utterly of what we have done, to forgive ourselves in the sense that God forgives us, and to accept understandingly the social consequences of our action. We may have to accept society's deterrent punishment and to look for society's forgiveness. For the remedial view of penology now emergent in western civilisation with its system of indefinite sentences and of discretionary parole, is just that: society offering forgiveness to the reformed. God can do no less.

God's 'cure for sin', then, is for each individual a new understanding of himself, of his relationship to his fellows, and of his relationship to God. 'Salvation' is the birth of a desire to rise above and beyond the inadequacy and poverty and joylessness of the past, and to live creatively, lovingly, increasingly. This the story of the life and death of Jesus engenders within us with unparallelled emotive power. Our belief that this particular human life was the one which God himself shared to the full, deepens and intensifies our recognition that this death is a challenge to us to live creatively, and to identify ourselves with God's unfolding purposes. The story of the life and death of Jesus wakens us out of personal self-absorption into living with and for others, and especially with and for God. This is indeed 'salvation'.

In the past, preachers often sought to induce a 'conviction of sin' and this was then healed by the offer of divine forgiveness set forth in the Cross. As a technique of personal therapy it was often amazingly effective. The eighteenth and nineteenth century movements known as the Evangelical Revivals, with all their potent influence on Western, particularly 'Anglo-Saxon' history, sprang very largely out of its widespread application. But the technique arose out of a system of ideas which do not consort with the current interpretation of the human situation. Mankind as a race is not to be thought of as a 'guilty' society. Human society must be recognised as imperfect, immature, gravely pathological, and highly precarious, but not guilty. When we remember the lowly origins of the species, especially when we recall the domination of blind instinct, which still wholly governs almost all of his fellow-creatures and against which man's own emergent intelligence has had to struggle and still has to struggle so painfully, human achievement far outweighs human failure. The fact that greed, slavery, race-hatred, war, still threaten to destroy mankind is not surprising, seeing the background out of which man has come.[7] What is surprising is that he has created modern technology, has built the Assouan Dam, has elaborated medical science, has constantly extended the rule of law, has conceived the Welfare State, has organised the United Nations, and has written the Oxford Book of English (or any other nation's) Verse. These are the significant things about the human animal. Well might Shakespeare exclaim: 'What a piece of work is man!'.

This may sound all very untheological, but it is true. That is, it reflects honestly the knowledge and insights of our day. It is consistent with the universally accepted hypothesis of evolution.[8] The concept of *Angst*, so beloved of some theologians, was borrowed from the post-war Germans, and is a

[7] Those who hold a pessimistic view of man's future are those who took a naive and unrealistic view of his past and so hoped that the Golden Age was already upon us. Two world wars and an economic depression produced a sharp reaction and induced the widespread pessimism among the so-called 'intellectuals' of our day. But a more sober estimate of man's past provides grounds for a realistic and cautious optimism with regard to his future.

[8] I realise that this type of thinking, put forward by F. R. Tennant as early as 1902, and again in 1912, (*The Concept of Sin*, Cambridge, 1912, esp. p. 151) has long since been 'discredited'; but in fact it was never refuted, it was merely disliked and dismissed. Given a belief in evolution rather than 'a Fall', and given a personal rather than a juridical concept of God, an interpretation of the concept of sin along the lines of Tennant's approach becomes inevitable. This is not to 'explain away' sin; it remains a fearful reality, and Hiroshima, Belsen and the slave-trade remind us grimly of it.

pathological concept. Theological guilt derives from an out-dated concept of God, and is seldom met with today. That is why in actual living we send anyone who is 'emotionally disturbed' not to a theologian but to a psychiatrist.[9] Paul, Augustine, Luther, Wesley, to quote the great names of evangelical tradition[10] suffered from a conviction of theological guilt in an acute form, and genuinely found release in the story of Jesus and his death—but we do not need to induce a disease simply because we know of a cure. I do not have to believe I am a condemned and guilty sinner, haled to confront an angry Deity, before the story of Jesus can grip and recreate me.

It may be said that I have obviously misinterpreted the doctrine of the atonement because my understanding of the cross has deprived it of its unique character. It is not simply a cavil to reply that since every man is unique and every event is unique, the death of Jesus and its significance for mankind must inevitably be unique. The claim that the death of Jesus is 'unique' is in itself a useless concept, simply because it is so evident. If it is meant that there are no other events in history of a like significance, the answer must be that this just is not true. The failing arctic explorer stumbling off into the blizzard in order to give his companions a chance to reach the next food depôt, the soldier accepting certain death to protect his company's retreat, Socrates drinking poison rather than betray his

---

But it does place sin within man's sphere of competence; it does become something which with God's help he can hope to overcome. It thus becomes properly the subject of moral appeal, as well as the ground of an offer of salvation. For a different but very sensitive estimate of Pennant cf. *The Meaning of Sin*, London, 1956, by my former colleague and Principal at Didsbury College, Frederic Greeves.

[9] This I have noticed is standard practice now not only on university campuses, but even in evangelical seminaries.

[10] It is significant that Jesus is never included among the great names of the 'evangelical' tradition. Guilt had in fact as little place in his thinking as sacrifice. This was however conveniently explained by the doctrines of the 'sinlessness' of Jesus and the 'immaculate conception' of Mary.

life-long advocacy of respect for law, these have all been, many times and often, used as parallel illustrations of the dying of Jesus, simply because they are parallel. The death of Jesus does not gain in significance from any 'uniqueness' which may be claimed for it. Its significance lies in the circumstance not that it is 'unique' in some way other facts are not 'unique', but rather in that it is an incident in human history, arising out of a situation such as *mutatis mutandis* we may well find ourselves in, and therefore it holds a challenge and an inspiration for us all. What gives the death of Jesus its quite outstanding emotive potency is that it was Jesus who died. Because he believed in God's purposes in the world, he lived as he did and he died as he did, and he is the example for us all.

And yet more than an example. Because 'God was in Christ', because, that is, this was the human life in which God participated and through which he expressed himself, the life and death of Jesus reveal a great deal about God himself. This was how God thought a man ought to live, and if need be, die. Because it was Jesus who lived and died for the Kingdom, we may be quite sure that the Kingdom is God's dream also. When we live, therefore, according to the teaching of Jesus and in the spirit of Jesus, we know that we are one with all the purposes of the universe. Physical, biological, cultural evolution all lead up to and are absorbed by the hope of the Kingdom. In the life and death of Jesus we have our one sure indication of what life is all about: it is about the Kingdom. That is why the most christian act of worship is to take bread and break it and eat it, to take wine and pour it and drink, in order to 'show forth the Lord's death'. That is why the christian, even though he goes alone, goes most reverently to church on Good Friday, the most christian day in all the year.

Jesus, I have suggested, believed he would be vindicated. Did that vindication take place when a believing Church arose, a vindication in the judgements and in the hearts of those who saw in him God's Messiah, or was there also an historical event, a physical resurrection? The New Testament affirms that Jesus not only died by crucifixion but also that he revived after death and returned to meet with and be recognised by his friends and disciples. Further, the New Testament, though extremely confused and divergent in the various resurrection narratives, is quite clear in its main points: the personal identity of the risen Christ with the historical Jesus; the physical aspect of this event, in that Jesus after the resurrection had a body which could be touched and handled; the identity of the body of Jesus after the resurrection with his body before death; and the fact that the tomb was empty.

It should be remembered that the Hebrews had a much more realistic view of human personality than had the Greeks. Whereas the Greeks thought of the soul as existing independently from the body, to which it was only temporarily linked by its sojourn in the world, the Hebrews recognised the body as the basis of personality, and a constituent part of individual human existence. The Greek view is summed up in the phrase 'the body the prison of the soul' and the Hebrew view in the phrase 'no body, no person'.[11] Hence the New Testament insistence that the resurrection of Jesus involved his body. When Paul discusses the hope of continued existence after death for individual followers of Jesus he is always careful to say two things: first, it will not be a bodiless existence; second, the resurrection body is related to, but not identical with, the physical body existent before death—in his famous paradoxical phrases the resurrected are to be 'clothed upon' with a 'spiritual body'.[12]

[11] These insights are primarily due to H. Wheeler Robinson's original studies of Hebrew psychology—cf. particularly 'Hebrew Psychology' in *The People and the Book*, ed. A. S. Peake, Oxford, 1925, pp. 353–382. They have been carried forward by other scholars, and J. A. T. Robinson's *The Body*, London, 1952, provides an interesting and challenging development of them.

[12] The important passages are 1 Corinthians 15:35–50, and 2 Corinthians 5:1–10.

To these concepts I bring three further ideas. First, that human existence (and that includes Jesus) cannot be thought of apart from an organ, 'the body'. Secondly, that it is conceivable, however, that the body, having by its organic complexity given rise first to cerebral and psychical identity, and then to self-awareness and finally personality, has thereby created something more permanent than itself. That is, that personality having once arisen and having broken out of what I earlier called 'the tyranny of the cortex', and having gained a limited control over body-functions, finally achieves an independence of them. It is conceivable that when the body dies, the personality, if it were sufficiently integrated and co-ordinated as a continuity of memory, possessing a sense of values and a will to achieve objectives, could survive the loss of the body by conceptualising its own identity as a replacement of the body. The man who has a leg amputated is often 'aware' of the missing limb for a long time after the operation. Perhaps this could serve as an analogy of the mind surviving the loss of the body by conceptualising its own integrated identity to take the place of the body. 'I' can continue as 'I' because 'I' think of myself as 'me'.[13]

It does not seem inherently inconsistent with the nature of this universe, in which the distinction between matter and force has resolved into a mathematical equation, that the physical body should set up a personal activity which is in fact the physical matter of the body translated into terms of force, and that this force could continue after the physical basis which originally gave rise to it has reverted to other forms of matter. This is the more conceivable when we recall that the body

[13] It is interesting to note that J. A. T. Robinson draws attention to Bultmann's account of 'Paul's understanding of *sōma* ("body") as "the self the object of its own consciousness or action"—the "me" rather than the "I",' citing *Theologie des N.T.*, I, p. 192 (*The Body*, pp. 12–13, note 1.). Robinson adds that such a way of thinking is 'essentially un-Hebrew and indeed post-Cartesian.' But then I am post-Cartesian.

itself is not a static phenomenon, but is a constantly changing complex of matter, with cells being born and dying by the million every day, and that its identity cannot be defined in purely physical terms. David Thomson used to say that a man literally hangs on to his identity by the skin of his teeth—tooth enamel being the one part of the body which is not in a continuous process of break-down and replacement.

To come back then to the resurrection of Jesus. In my understanding of God and the universe, the resurrection of Jesus, if it is to be considered a fact, must be consonant with the general functions of matter and mind. The old idea of miracle as an interruption or abrogation of natural patterns will not serve us here any more than it does elsewhere. It is, however, consonant with what we know of the physical aspect of reality, and with what I at least understand by personality, to think Jesus of Nazareth was so fully co-ordinated and integrated as a person that when his bodily organism was destroyed, his identity survived and that he made himself known to his followers. Whether at first he may have returned to and made use of his physical body—as other men have reactivated their body after two or three minutes of clinical death— but that speedily the body was laid aside and Jesus' conceptualisation of his body was made apparent to his friends and followers, are speculations which it seems profitless to pursue.

These ideas, it seems to me, provide for a conceivable view of the resurrection of Jesus, and would account for the two central phenomena—his appearances to his followers and the emptiness of the tomb. This last I take to be as sure a fact as any that historical research can establish: if the tomb had not been empty the Jewish or Roman authorities would have been quick to display the body of Jesus and put a stop to this rumour that he was still alive. Nor can I think that any one among the disciples was hiding the body away; the measure of deceit is too great to contemplate.[14] Unless the whole resurrection story is pure myth (and incidentally myths never are pure) then the tomb was empty and the disciples believed they had met with Jesus, alive after death.

Given the person Jesus was, I myself am prepared to believe that he survived death and that he continues now, free from physical limitations, and available personally to those who seek knowledge of him. I am also prepared to speculate (as I have done above) on how this might happen though I am certainly in no position to be dogmatic. The value of these speculations is only to assure me that what I believe is not unreasonable. But my reason for being prepared even to contemplate the possibility of the resurrection lies wholly elsewhere. It is not because I think Jesus needs that kind of vindication. The recognition of his supreme worth in the hearts and minds of his followers is all the vindication he needs. But I find I cannot entertain the thought that what he was, and what he meant to God, dissolved with the physical dissolution of his body. Rather, I believe that in some manner I cannot fathom, he is still he, and is indeed still the Lord of his Church. The resurrection stories in the New Testament clearly owe much to legend-making influences, but nevertheless I think they point us to a significant truth: Jesus lives. He himself, when asked about the after-life, referred to the nature of God. God, he said, is not the God of the dead, but of the living.[15] So, too, I am persuaded that if God is what I believe him to be, then so bright and precious a personality as that of Jesus can not have wholly terminated when his physical body could function no more. I believe he lives, and I have faith in him.

[14] The discussion of this point in *Who Moved the Stone?* by Frank Morison, New York and London, 1930, I still find quite convincing; cf. pp. 127–173. For a discussion of the theology of the resurrection see Michael Ramsey's small but very valuable book *The Resurrection of Christ*, London, 1945. A. M. Ramsey, now Archbishop of Canterbury, was at the time of writing Professor of Divinity in Durham University.

[15] Matthew 22:32.

But there is one very important point still to be made. The New Testament proposes Jesus as the God-man because he returned to life after death. Peter in the Pentecost speech said that Jesus was clearly the Messiah because he had been raised from the dead: 'This Jesus God raised up, and of that we are all witnesses.' Paul on Mars Hill said God would judge the world 'by a man whom he has appointed, and of this he has given assurance to all men by raising him from the dead.'[16] The New Testament message is that Jesus is Son of God, that he is Messiah, and that as authentication of this he was raised from the dead—believe in him and accept him as Lord. My own version of the Gospel is that I so respond to his teaching and person as to call him Lord and Master, and therefore find it possible to believe that he is the God-man who survived death and continues alive and is available to us in this generation. I am then a christian, but not a New Testament christian. It was right and proper that in the first century men should say 'Jesus is alive; you can believe this, because I assure you I have seen him.' But that kind of witness, whether first-hand or enshrined in scripture, is no longer convincing. The only faith I can have in Jesus is one I have gained for myself—from his teaching, from the records of his life, and the manner of his dying and from the impact of his personality upon mine. The result of my encounter with him is such that I can believe that such a man could even survive the physical catastrophe of death. From this basis of belief, I can launch out into the great adventure of faith—seeking to know him in prayer and worship. *Christianus sum.* Therefore my last chapter must be a discussion of the ways in which a christian, having discovered where he stands and having come to the christian understanding of his situation, now tries to live in accordance with that understanding.

[16] Acts 2:32 and 17:31.

Chapter Eight

THE PRACTICE OF RELIGION

'WE go,' said Mr Squeers, 'upon the practical mode of teaching, Nickleby; the regular education system. C-l-e-a-n, clean, verb active, to make bright, to scour. W-i-n, win, d-e-r, der, winder, a casement. When the boy knows this out of the book, he goes and does it.' Religion is, in Mr Squeers's sense of the term, the most practical of all philosophies. Essentially, it is not an intellectual argument; it is an experience, both proceeding from and issuing in a way of life.

Anyone who has moved outside his own culture must be aware of the widespread fact of religious experience. In the literature of the Japanese sects of Buddhism, in the poems of the *bhakti* sects of Hinduism, in the writings of *sufi* movements in Islam, in the hasidist tradition in Judaism, in the letters of the Spanish christian mystics, there is, to quote but a few examples, ample evidence of the reality and the power of those experiences of the human personality, which have been engendered by the practices and ideas of religion.[1] Indeed,

---

[1] The current fashion of employing psychedelic drugs to facilitate such experiences is nothing new. It is indeed very ancient—*haoma* in ancient Persian religion, *soma* and *hashish* in Indian religions are well-known examples, as indeed were the sulphur fumes which were inhaled by the Delphic oracle. The important question is whether those who resort to these drugs do so as a means of reaching a spiritual reality exterior to their own personality, or whether they are content to be exploring the abnormal

many students of religion (and I am one among them) would say that until an observer has so identified with a religion that he can imaginatively enter into the religious experience of its adherents, he has not begun to understand it. Speaking of the current phrase 'the death of God', Wilfred Cantwell Smith remarks that the words function as a symbol, indeed an ultimate religious symbol, and continues: 'First, it is sacred; and second, it is therefore translucent. Those for whom it is sacred, when they look at it do not, like the rest of us, see it, but see through it to something beyond—something not precise, not objective, not finite. It is not something that they see, perhaps, so much as something about which they feel—and feel deeply. Its form serves as a highly charged crystallizing of whatever emotions or insights or sense of ultimacy it can be made to carry for those who treat it as absolute. To understand it—just as to understand the syllable OM for hindus, or the Qur'an for muslims, or any myth—one must ask oneself how much transcendence it can be made to carry for those who have chosen its particular shape to represent the pattern of their religiousness.'[2] Similarly, to understand the mysticism of St John of the Cross one must surrender to the experience of 'the dark night of the soul'; to appreciate the significance of Zen Buddhism one must oneself live with, and wrestle with, one of the classical *koan* or riddles with which the Master teases, exhausts and finally breaks down the spiritual defensiveness of the disciple; to

---

functioning of their own mental processes. In either case, the practice seems to me exceedingly dangerous, for in matters of religion a man needs all his wits about him: religion can be personally and socially uplifting, or it can be stultifying and even positively evil. A man must therefore be able to appraise his own religion honestly, and to derange one's critical faculties just when one needs them most seems to me a highly reprehensible thing to do. But it has to be recognised that the first intention, however misguided, is at least a serious endeavour; the second is mere sensationalism, as sterile and self-imprisoned as masturbation, to which indeed it is a spiritual parallel. But the present fashion is, one gathers, wholly of this second kind.

[2] *Questions of Religious Truth*, 1967, p. 16.

appreciate the Hebrew psalter, one must identify with the experience of social and spiritual ostracism, and the sense of deliverance and renewal which come with 'salvation'.

It is then in no way unusual that in the form of christianity in which I have been brought up, I am confronted not only with an intellectual interpretation of the human situation, but also with a religious experience, and a challenge to pay the price to enter into that experience.[3] There would be something seriously amiss if this were not so. Nevertheless I have to add that nothing concerning religion is so objectionable and dissuasive to thoughtful men and women of my generation, both within and without the Church, as the ill-informed and insensitive attempts of some evangelically-minded enthusiasts to thrust upon others their own understanding and apprehension of that experience. The greatest limitation in the thinking of John Wesley, understandable in terms of the age in which he lived but nevertheless a disability from which his followers even in this generation are still finding it difficult to discumber themselves, was his assumption that the Methodist variety of christian religious experience was a pattern to which all men must conform. His analysis of that experience provided the structure of his remarkable production *A Collection of Hymns for the Use of the People called Methodists* and was presumed to depict the normative progress of the truly christian soul: 'Exhorting Sinners to Return to God', 'Describing Formal Religion', 'Describing Inward Religion', 'Praying for Repentance, 'Mourners Convinced of Sin', 'For Believers Rejoicing',

---

[3] The classical accounts of the Methodist understanding of christian religious experience is to be found in the *Sermons* of John Wesley. (Works, Third Edition, London, 1833, Vols. 4–8) and even more so in the hymns of Charles Wesley; but the six volumes of *Lives of Early Methodist Preachers*, ed. Thomas Jackson, Third Edition, London, 1865–66, were collected from the early numbers of the Arminian Magazine and are particularly informative and descriptive.

'For Believers Fighting', 'For Believers Seeking for Full Redemption', 'For Believers Saved', 'For Believers Interceding for the World'. The attempt to force all men and women, and especially young people brought up in a strongly christian home, into that one mould of conviction of sin and catharsis through conversion has done, together with much good, very great harm. But of the reality and power of the experience of 'salvation' to which Wesley and his followers have testified, a serious student of the subject can be in no doubt. But what is here said of Wesley's *Hymns* and the 'evangelical experience' must also be said of Bunyan's *Pilgrim's Progress* and the Puritan experience, and again of the New Testament document, the Letter to the Romans, and of the experience of 'salvation' which it delineates. For Paul's potent little work is also an analysis of his own religious experience, and a rationalisation of it in terms of a systematic theology, and an offer of that analysis as the definitive description of the human situation vis-à-vis the divine power of the universe. As perceptive and richly informative classics of the christian religion I receive and honour these great works; I do not, however, believe that any one of them speaks for all men in all times. Parts of the Letter to the Romans speak to me and for me—I am thinking particularly of the first, the eighth and the thirteenth chapters—but a great deal of the Letter I can only read historically.

Nevertheless, in whatever terms it may be described, I am aware that Christianity not only interprets for me the human situation but it also offers me a religiously significant experience and I have therefore to review that experience and attempt to put it into my own words and give it my own expression. It goes without saying that if I have denied universality to Paul I certainly do not claim it for myself. We each of us see reality from our own viewpoint, 'as in a mirror, darkly', and each of us can only describe as much as he can see.

For myself, I have to say two things: First, the acceptance of the christian account of the human situation has meant for me a sense of liberation. It has freed me from a sense of bewilderment as to who I am, and of frustration, as to what I should be doing; it has related me meaningfully to this physical and lively universe, and it has given me personal goals in daily living. As a result of my christian faith, I know why I am I, and I know what I am trying to achieve. I am, to recapitulate briefly, a physical-mental organism, which was produced by the physical and biological forces of the universe by means of the process we call evolution, and to which, by reason of a self-awareness, the quality of life we call personal is possible; my business in life, then, is to become more and more of a person, that is, to relate appreciatively to the universe, to relate positively and creatively to my fellows, and to relate wholly and without reserve to God. This last brings me to my second affirmation.

Acceptance of the christian account of the human situation opens the way to an experience of personal awareness of God who is himself, as I understand it, the personal quality of the universe. The nub of the judaeo-christian inheritance lies in two sayings from the Testaments: from the Old, the opening words of the most meaningful of all the psalms, 'Lord, Thou hast searched me and known me'; and from the New the words of Paul, 'I know him in whom I have believed'. The claim to be in personal communion with God, to be known and to know, is quite basic and fundamental to the practice of the christian religion. If a man cannot say, 'I believe I have communion with God, and that God has communion with me', he is no christian. But if that is all he says, he is no christian. To be truly christian he will go on to say, 'I believe that Jesus of Nazareth was not destroyed by the experience of death but is a living personality so identified with God that when I have communion with God, I have communion with him, and when God draws near to me, it is through the personality of Jesus that he does so. My communion is with the Father through the Son.'[4]

I discussed the historical aspects of the christian belief in the resurrection of Jesus in a previous chapter. Here I need to add that this belief in the continued life and fully personal existence of Jesus, and in his availability to all who turn to him, and his identity with God who is the life of the universe, is the heart and soul of the christian religion. The christian affirms with all his being 'I have fellowship with Jesus and through him I have fellowship with God'. Despite all the intellectual difficulties in formulating the doctrine, he believes in the incarnation (that is that Jesus was or became one with God) because he experiences the reality of communion with Jesus, and through Jesus with God. Incarnation and resurrection are the two great parts of what a christian means when he says 'I believe in Jesus Christ'; the third and complementary part is that Jesus is Saviour and therefore Lord.

This is the form of christian truth, and the expression of it, in which I was brought up, which I have carefully re-examined, and which I am now wholeheartedly prepared to reaffirm. I believe that Jesus is personally alive today and is available to those who recognise him as Master and Lord. I believe that to be aware of him and to be in conscious communion with him is to experience a renewal and re-invigoration of one's life. Like the New Testament, Christianity has never quite known whether to identify the continuing Jesus of the resurrection with the concept of the Holy Spirit, or whether to distinguish between them, for while in theory there is distinction (as in the doctrine of the triune being of God) in practice the two have been fairly well identified. But of the reality of a divine presence available to men and women in every age, there has been in

---

[4] He should also to be true to the classical christian tradition add 'by the Spirit'. But I do not wish to be distracted at the moment from my main argument; there is a further brief comment below.

christian witness no doubt whatsoever. It is this conviction which makes Christianity a gospel rather than a philosophy.

What the Christian further believes is that when a man responds to the challenge of the historical life and death and resurrection of Jesus, and seeks to enter the Kingdom and to live by its ideals, he is not left to battle out his existence alone. Rather, he receives the co-operation of the Holy Spirit (or the continuing person of Jesus) which gives him a new vitality in the human situation. I have come to terms with the idea of incarnation partly by means of the concept which I called 'symbiosis', that is, the idea of God experiencing a human life by identification with that observing centre of conscience which arose out of the physical organism born of a girl called Mary and named Jesus bar-Joseph. It now seems to me that in some way analogous to that, we can invite the continuing person of Jesus, himself so intimately at one with God, to enter into the same kind of identity-relationship with us. The experience from the human side is of a dropping of the barriers of individuality, it is a surrender of the ego of one's own personality to the entry of the divine person of Jesus. It is indeed for most of us an attitude of mind only as yet very partially achieved, and one which has constantly to be renewed. I myself can only liken its effects to raising the window blinds in a dark house on a bright, sunny morning. Charles Wesley's morning hymn has always for that reason greatly appealed to me and I have said or sung it to myself on countless mornings, in fact most days for many years:

> *Christ, whose glory fills the sky,*
>   *Christ, the true and only light,*
> *Sun of righteousness, arise,*
>   *Triumph o'er the shades of night.*
>   *Day-star from on high, be near,*
>   *Day-star, in my heart appear.*

If this, then, is an attempted description of the christian experience of religion as one raised in the evangelical tradition understands it, the question arises as to how it is to be translated intelligently into habits of daily living. By reason of the Anglican-Wesleyan tradition I became in my teens and twenties tolerably well-acquainted with the classical tradition of christian prayer: Thomas à Kempis, Bishop Andrewes, Loyola's *Spiritual Exercises*, and among more modern writings, Bede Frost's *The Art of Mental Prayer*. While still having a deep appreciation for these classical patterns of prayer, I have moved far from their prescriptions, since they do not sufficiently allow for the conditions of our age, but I nevertheless still partake of many of their mental attitudes. This book is not intended to be one of personal confession, except in so far as it is necessary to make clear my religious affirmation: suffice it then to say that after a period in which I abandoned the practice on rational grounds, I have come back strongly to believe that a man, particularly a busy man, needs to renew each day, at least once a day, his relationship with the transcendent. How he does it, whether by a Daily Office or by free meditation, is his affair. But to take time each day, to recall and to strengthen one's self in the Fifth Dimension which is God, is quite necessary. What often puzzles me about so many of my colleagues and acquaintances is that they can have such a generous awareness of truth and goodness and beauty and not feel a need to relate that experience to anything beyond the seventy years and the historical accidents of a purely psycho-physical experience. I may be very wrong, and they may have resources of which I am not aware, but they seem to me to be neglecting to hear the orchestration of life's theme; they appear to be content to take life 'penny-plain' when they could experience it 'twopence coloured'. Faith, and its corollary prayer, so it seems to me, give life a stereoscopic depth, lacking which it is flat and superficial.

Worship I find equally significant but rather more difficult to cope with. The social witness of worship, the educative value for on-coming generations, the expression of the corporate life of the Church which is the incipient Kingdom of God, all these make public worship an obligation from which no one can regularly excuse himself on the grounds that he has more important things to do. That her majesty the Queen, and that many of her cabinet ministers in all her dominions, and that judges and eminent surgeons and university administrators and hard-pressed business men, find time to attend public worship is a sign of spiritual health. When highly-placed persons in any society—the school teacher in the village, the lawyer in the small town, the professor in the suburb-community, the Prime Minister in the capital—assume that while others should go to church they must attend to more urgent claims, ultimate values have already been placed in jeopardy.

Moreover, in a pattern of prayer and hymn, of psalm and scripture, of music and action and spoken word, there is the opportunity to weave a tapestry of great and satisfying beauty. It may seem a far cry from Verdi's *Requiem Mass* or Mattins in St Paul's to the 'do-it-yourself' service in a country chapel, but I have known the joy and the renewal of worship in many lands and in many languages and in an infinite variety of forms. Isaac Watts was speaking soberly when, concerning worship, he spoke of those things which 'make this duty our delight'.

The problem is, however, that the reality and the ideal seldom coincide, and one is left wondering why. Two reasons suggest themselves to me and perhaps they resolve into one. The first is the lack of expectancy among so many worshippers; they come expecting to be bored and are not disappointed. The second is I believe more serious. Until well after the Second World War, the rank and file of the Church were culturally undisturbed, and references to golden crowns as symbolic of peace, or to sin-sick souls as indicative of their own unhappiness, or even to resting forever on Jesus' breast, were not taken seriously amiss. Now, however, there has been a swift change in thought-forms. Even more than the making of the atom bomb, or the discovery of DNA, or any other of the scientific and technological strides of the past twenty years, the hoisting of Sputnik, and the space-travels of the astronauts have I believe profoundly affected the thinking of ordinary men and women. Overnight, man became a creature of space, and science-fiction became the new mythology. Reality is always expressed in myth, and until the 1950's the great majority of western men and women had found the biblical mythology barely but just sufficient. Now, however, those thought-forms are no longer natural to us, and yet our scriptures, our liturgies and above all our hymns are written in their language. The Bible as a whole continues to be significant, and many of its passages can still be read in church without too much demand on the hearer; consciously or unconsciously he is doing a simultaneous translation of what he hears into the terms in which he thinks, and for many passages this is not too difficult. Even so, large parts of the Prophets, and of the Epistles, are now too far removed from modern concepts and should no longer be imposed on normal congregations. Their minds simply idle while the meaningless syllables roll over their heads. The Bible can only be used selectively in contemporary worship: the old notion of a lectionary which took the congregation regularly through the whole of the Old Testament and New Testament once a year or every three years has lost its validity. Liturgies can be discerningly rewritten, though this is a much harder task than anyone who has not attempted it can imagine. It is easy to produce a flat prose; the problem is to achieve the undated vocabulary, the terseness of thought, the balanced rhythm of phrase, which are characteristic of good liturgy, and still remain within ear-shot of a congregation raised on newspapers and television. But nowhere is re-writing so urgently needed as in the hymn-book. Some have gone so far as to say that the hymn was an 18th century device which has no place in the twentieth; historically this is not true, and I think it is not perceptive of the future. Group singing shows no sign of losing its attractiveness, and the power of a song to express a faith, first exploited it is said by Arius in the third century, has been in recent times exemplified afresh by the blending of the current interest in 'folk-songs' with the struggle for racial equality the world over. But the need for hymns which neither offend modern taste nor mock modern intelligence is a matter of great importance.[5] The Christian Church will, I believe, very largely depend for its fortunes over the next half century on its ability to re-fashion and make relevant its congregational worship.[6] However, my point here is that an essential element in the practice of religion is engaging in its public exercises, and that therefore as a christian, I have an obligation to go to church, 'on the Lord's day, in the Lord's house, with the Lord's people'. Out of that participation in worship have grown religious, cultural and social associations, which are indeed on any sober estimate among my most valuable assets.

The third element which I believe to be basic in the practice of religion is that of self-discipline. This has shown itself in many guises down through the ages, from the observance in the

[5] I am myself working on a revision of the congregational Psalter for the United Church of Canada, and I am looking forward with great hopes to the new Hymnary now being prepared by order of the General Council of that Church, in co-operation with the Anglican Church of Canada. But the tasks are not ones to be easily accomplished.

[6] Wyclif's English Bible and Luther's German Bible, and Vatican II's authorisation of the Canon of the Mass in the vernacular are among the most significant events in church-history. They are a disavowal of the false mystery of the unintelligible—a Coptic christian service in Cairo comes vividly to mind—in favour of an intelligent understanding of religion. Mumbo-jumbo however sacred is still mumbo-jumbo and neither sentiment nor conservatism should be allowed to entice us into its trap. Even so, the rawly-new is very unsatisfying liturgically, for the language of worship should be richly evocative. Perhaps the best rule in liturgical reform is 'little and often'.

173

early church of Wednesday and Friday as *dies stationum*, when the christian stood to his post, to the days of abstinence and the observance of Advent and Lent in traditional catholicism, and the unremitting abstinence of the Puritans, who believed that the warfare in which they were engaged allowed for no remission. The need for some form of self-discipline is as evident today as ever, but the discipline should be freely chosen, and largely self-designated, since ecclesiastical systems always fail in their intentions. But of the continuing need for self-ordering, self-determining, there can be no doubt. In an affluent society it is becoming a very difficult matter to make use of what technology so abundantly provides, without becoming addicted to the appurtenances of 'gracious living' to the point where all else must be surrendered for them. Clearly, we still have to imitate Paul, who knew both how to abound and how to be in want, both how to possess all things and how to possess nothing, but this is more easily said than done. It is equally difficult, in an age when the sexual mores are changing so fast, to know where one stands oneself and even more how one should advise one's children. But that the wholesomeness of family life and the personal values of marriage should be strongly respected remains as true as ever. The problem is to translate these general convictions into consistent patterns of day-to-day living.

I am convinced of two things which I believe will remain stable whatever else changes. First, that to be religious includes as an essential feature a sense of spiritual ambition. The truly religious man is not content with what he is, but seeks all his life to grow more mature, more wise, more fully-human as the years pass. He hopes to attain a deeper knowledge of himself and of his own potentialities, and to learn how to control and develop the forces within his own nature. He hopes to come to a more creative relationship with his fellow men and women, and constantly to discover a richer enjoyment in his association with them. He hopes also to achieve a broader entrance into beauty, and into culture in all its rich variety of forms and media, and to gain a more comprehensive appreciation of the universe and of the mysterious life-force within it. By all these means he hopes to come day by day to a truer insight into the nature of God and even one day to know why he was made for God, and why he can find ultimate satisfaction only in him. He stands and he seeks to understand.

If, then, a religious man should always be striving, always seeking a further goal, the second thing of which I am sure is that for the christian there are no rules. Paul said perhaps more than he understood when he told his very new and very perplexed converts 'for freedom Christ has set us free'.[7] He meant specifically that christians were set free from the trammels of the Mosaic law, with its obligation of circumcision and its burden of food and ritual taboos. But the fact is that in christian ethics there never have been any rules, only principles. How to behave with regard to work and the sense of vocation, with regard to material affluence, to entertainment, to politics, to racial relations, to international affairs; how to relate to persons, to other members of the family, and to colleagues, to those for whom you are responsible and those to whom you are responsible; how to respond positively to those who frustrate and harm you, and how to be grateful to those who help you generously—these are the complex issues of life and the christian must play every situation wholly by ear. To be an intelligent christian is to know that there are no rules. There are indeed guidelines. One of the most important of them, perhaps the most important of them, is that one should as much as possible treat men and women as persons and not as things. Inevitably we are all reduced at times to being merely one name among many on a list, to being a bare statistic among the results of a questionnaire, or to being a 'case', whether it is of

[7] Galatians 5:1.

175

appendicitis or of illegal parking, and it is equally inevitable that we have to deal with other men and women quite often at that level. We could not get through our working day if we did not. But the truly christian insight is always to be ready to recognise the individual who needs to be treated as a person, and to do so whenever it is possible. This art ranges all the way from giving one's order courteously to a waitress in a busy restaurant to devoting all the time one can spare from essential duties to a colleague whose wife is undergoing a dangerous and doubtful operation; but there is no attitude or practice which makes so great a difference to all else in life as this. Jesus called it by its Old Testament name of 'loving your neighbour as yourself', and further described it as doing to others what you hope they would do for you. Coupled with an understanding that you are a creature in a vast universe, inherent in which is a mighty purpose, and that your rôle is to seek to grasp and to co-operate with that purpose—traditionally this is called 'loving God'—, this principle of 'loving one's neighbour' embraces all christian ethical teaching. Indeed, the two principles so blend that no one has ever spoken more profoundly on the art of christian living than Augustine when he said 'Love God and do what you like'. A great deal of the zest of life arises from discovering new ways of putting that principle into practice.

Prayer, worship, the christian pattern of living—my experience has been that these add up to an intelligent, meaningful and rewarding way of life. I have never heard of one better. But at this point a large question raises itself, and cannot be evaded. To remain satisfying, the christian stance must relate itself to reality. It cannot be just a pleasing construct, an agreeable system of make-believe. The question then is this: can I honestly believe that in a vast universe of solar systems and galaxies, or even on a planet housing nearly two billion human beings, I as an individual can have any personal significance with God? Is it not merely pietistic self-delusion to speak of 'talking with him', or of having a personal relationship with him? I believe not: or rather I should say, in view of all the difficulties involved, 'I dare to believe it is not so'. I return to where I began: The universe produced me; the universe produced me to be a person; therefore the universe—God— must treat me as a person, and that means knowing me as an individual and being concerned with my personal affairs. I am not so naive as to think that I can pray for good weather to favour my personal pursuits, or to ask that the physical chain of cause and effect should be interrupted for my convenience; nevertheless I believe that I may with all humility but with all propriety ask for God's concern in my attempts to cope with my existential situation and to live life at an increasingly personal level. How each one of us makes the conviction that God has a personal concern for him the basis of his daily living will depend on his upbringing, his degree of sophistication, his sense of what is beautiful, on a hundred and one personal conditions: but I hold on to the belief that it is a conviction in which each one of the millions of human beings can legitimately share.

With all our philosophy and technology we remain emotionally very anthropomorphic in our thinking about God. Because we cannot conceive of ourselves being able to be personally aware of, and personally concerned with, more than a very small circle of friends and acquaintances, and because in our dealings with one another, the multiplication of numbers inevitably means the reduction of the individual to a less than personal level, we feel that God must suffer from the same limitation. Intellectually we realise that God must transcend our limitations; emotionally we are sure he cannot. The rôle of myth in the ancient world was, in part at least, to meet and satisfy these emotional needs of the mind; the function of a myth was to reduce the racial, the generic, down to the individual and the particular, so that a vast problem became of a size the mind could handle. Thus in the Garden of

Eden myth, all human nature in its relation with God is reduced to a single pair, Adam and Eve; in the story of Cain and Abel, the clash of personality is reduced to a quarrel between two brothers. We similarly need our myths and if in relation to this particularly important problem I refer to the computer, it is not because it 'proves' or 'explains' anything, but simply because it can perhaps serve as our myth. A time-shared computer on a university campus has many terminals. The computer itself may be located in the Engineering building, but the terminals may be in the University Library, the School of Business, the Chemistry Building, or they may be downtown, or they may be a hundred, two hundred miles away, linked by long-distance telephone. At any time, day or night, from any one of these terminals, a problem may be posed and an answer required, and the response which any caller receives is that of instantaneous service and the effect is to place the whole of the resources of the computer at his disposal.[8] This is no analogy of the Divine Mind, but for some of us it may provide the kind of contemporary myth we need. It may reduce the problem to a size we can handle, it may enable us to believe, what I think a christian is committed to believe: that God is concerned with each of us as an individual, that he knows us by name, that he has a personal concern for each of us.

This, I think, is another of, perhaps the last of, the sticking points of religious faith. We can ponder and consider and rationalise but in the end, we are pushed to this point and faced with the alternative: will we or will we not believe? Long ago I

[8] What actually happens is that the computer, which will undoubtedly be working on a time-demanding major problem, will switch from that to deal with A; if call B comes in it will drop A and attend to B and C, and so on up to fifty, sixty calls according to its capacity. In the intervals of picking up new calls it reverts momentarily to its major problem, as well as going back to call A and B etc. in rotation. But the switches are achieved in microseconds, so that any particular user gets the impression of instant, uninterrupted service, with a maximum delay of perhaps six or seven seconds if the computer is really busy.

realised that religious belief is a matter, for me at least, of deliberate choice. I could either believe in a universe in which God is, and in which God has a concern for me, or I could believe in one which has resulted from 'a chance collocation of atoms' and in which I am just an unhappy accident. Almost literally, you pay your money and you take your choice. I pay the price in terms of a searching, critical enquiry leading to informed belief, and that gives me the freedom to have faith. I choose to believe in God who knows me and is concerned for me. I believe that Jesus is God expressing himself in terms of human personality. Therefore I can have faith in God and his Christ. Belief is the price you pay in order to have faith.

I still have two last questions. When I die, what will become of me? Frankly, I do not know. It is not inconceivable, as I said earlier when speaking of the resurrection of Jesus, that human personality can become independent of the physical organism which occasioned it. It may be that I shall be I in the presence of God through all eternity. On the other hand, it may be that there is more truth at this point in the insights of Hinduism and Buddhism. We Westerners perhaps over-rate the value of individuality, and it may be that salvation lies in escape from particularity into the Unity of Being, as the rain-drop returns to the ocean. Possibly the desire to be 'I' for ever, is itself immature. I do not know, and I am content to leave the matter in God's hands. What I do know is that my personal significance will not be lost, in the sense of being destroyed. I shall be caught up into the unity of the Church Triumphant, or into the unity of God; but whether these are two ways of saying the same thing I do not know. Jesus is reported as saying: 'I came that they may have life and have it more abundantly'. I have known that to be true here. He has introduced me to the Fifth Dimension and given all reality a stereoscopic depth which without him it lacks. I am prepared, therefore, to trust him with regard to my friends and loved-ones who have already passed through the experience of death, and I hope I may have the faith and the courage to trust him with myself when I in my turn come to die. I find my Easter faith expressed very simply but very adequately in some lines of John Greenleaf Whittier:

> *I know not where his islands lift*
> *Their fronded palms in air,*
> *I only know I cannot drift*
> *Beyond his love and care.*

I mentioned Hinduism and Buddhism, and that leads into the other last question. In this account of the christian understanding of the human situation, must I make an exclusive claim to the truth about God? When I began this enquiry I said 'In another generation the search for ultimate truth may be resumed. For this generation we have I think to recognise that Christianity is a myth, an interpretation of reality'.[9] I compared the use of 'myth' to the current use in the social and natural sciences of the term 'model'. I think we have now to recognise that to speak of God as a Person and of Jesus as the expression of God in terms of human personality is to speak in accordance with the christian 'model' or 'myth' of reality. When in the *Phaedo*, Socrates spoke of the other world which awaits the souls of men released from the restraints of the body in this world, he added: 'Now it would ill become a man of sense to insist that things are exactly as I have described them: but that this or something like it is true about our souls and their dwellings, since the soul is plainly immortal—this, in my opinion it is right to say, and it is worthwhile to risk the belief that it is so—for it is a noble venture—and such are the magic words which one should murmur over himself'.[10] That is, that

[9] See above p. 26.
[10] *Plato: Socratic Dialogues*, translated by W. D. Woodhead, Edinburgh 1953, pp. 175–177 (A114D).

instead of trusting in the amuletary words of the mystery cults, one should place confidence in the considered words of reasonable enquiry. For me then, the 'noble venture' is to affirm the considered words of christian faith: 'I dare believe in Jesus' name'.[11] But I cannot affirm that my christian understanding is the only model of truth, the only myth of reality. I have met personally and through their writings, too many good and wise men of other faiths and other traditions to be prepared to do that, even for a brief moment. I know that my christian account of man's situation brings rationality, meaning and purpose into my living. I believe it brings me into intimate relation with, to use Tillich's phrase, the Ground of Being. But I can readily accept that for an earnest muslim, a devout jew, a committed buddhist, a thoughtful hindu, their roads also may lead to reality. Each has indeed much to teach the other. We need to talk freely and at length before we can understand how our apparently mutually exclusive faiths relate to one another in the unity of truth. As C. J. Bleeker has so perceptively written: 'those who believe can afford to wait. . . . The logic of truth which God has revealed to mankind is sweeping us irresistibly towards a condition in which all true believers will be able to understand and appreciate each other's values, without having to relinquish the particular faith which is so dear to them.'[12] There may be many paths to the truth; I am content to affirm that Christianity is one of them.

I am constrained, however, as I think of Christianity in comparison with and indeed in some senses in competition with the other great faiths of mankind, Judaism, Islam, Hinduism,

[11] Cf. Charles Wesley:
> Surrounded by a host of foes,
> Stormed by a host of foes within,
> Nor swift to flee, nor strong to oppose,
> Single, against hell, earth and sin,
> Single yet undismayed I am:
> I dare believe in Jesu's name!

[12] *Christ in Modern Athens*, Leiden, 1965, p. 152.

Buddhism, to make again explicit what has indeed been implicit in this whole study; and that is, that a Christianity which attempts to commend itself as based upon an interruption of the natural order of the universe will be at a crippling disadvantage in that competition. The idea of a universe of natural order, emergent, evolving and uniform, from the microcosm of the atom on this and every other planet to the macrocosm of the furthest galaxies in space, a natural order, moreover, which expresses itself in all forms of matter, in all species of plant and animal life, and not least in the intelligent processes of man's thinking, has become the accepted, unchallengeable premise of all our thinking.[13] Because we live in a scientific age, this concept conditions all other ideas. Viewed from within, Christianity has seemed to many theologians, Karl Barth being the prime and venerable example, to derive its strength and its appeal to men from a claim to a superiority over that natural order, and from its presentation of the incarnation as a divine irruption into the affairs of men. Viewed from without, a standpoint which as I said in the Preface I have found myself involuntarily sharing these past few years, it is now quite clear that Christianity's one hope of continuing to capture the minds of men and to enlist their loyalty lies in its ability to present itself not as an interruption of the natural

[13] 'In Newton's age, for example, the world was conveniently divided into two mutually exclusive types of events. While some were accepted as supernatural and hence unintelligible, the majority of events were coming to be regarded as purely natural and hence as, in principle at least, open to human understanding. But the contemporary scientific view is much more radical. On essentially methodological grounds it discards the concept of the supernatural and resolves to treat all events as wholly natural. It proposes to treat all events as, in the final analysis, expressions of one single pattern. Indeed it regards any theory or hypothesis as adqeuate just to the extent to which it finds room for every conceivable event . . . every single scientist with whom I have discussed the question uses and reports himself as using such concepts . . . I simply do not see how it is possible to do science or better, how it is possible to "justify" it, on the other basis.' Alastair McKinnon, ' "Miracle" and "Paradox" ', *American Philosophical Quarterly*, Vol. 4, No. 4, October 1967, pp. 308–314.

order, but as a meaningful interpretation of it. So long as Christianity clings to the idea of miracle as that which is anomalous in a world of natural order, and bases its claims for consideration on the miraculous nature of the incarnation and the resurrection, and the consequent 'objective' interpretation of the atonement, it will appear to the best minds of our times naive and credulous, and as arising out of the fantasy-making and wish-fulfilment processes of the human psyche. This is a disability from which the other major religions are far more emancipated than are the popular forms of Christianity, so that it is easier and much more customary for a scientist to remain loyal to his religion if he is a jew or a muslim or a buddhist, than if he is a christian. This is particularly and significantly true in the fields of psychology and psychiatry, but it is noticeably so in all the social and natural sciences. Nevertheless, I am myself persuaded that an honest and coherent presentation of Christianity, and one true to the divine intention as it has been made clear to us in these days, can be made, and in such a way as to be true to its past and to secure its great and healthful influences for the future. Such a presentation would be loyal to the scriptures in general, but particularly to the spirit of the Wisdom Teaching of the Old and New Testaments and to the Johannine reinterpretation of the Gospel, and would also stand in the noble tradition of Clement of Alexandria, Origen, the Aristotelian synthesis, Abelard, the Anglican and Lockian inheritance of the Wesleys and of Bishop Butler, the open-mindedness of Charles Kingsley and the great biblical scholars of the nineteenth and twentieth centuries, and also of men in our own day as disparate in denomination and as unanimous in spirit as Harry Emerson Fosdick and Pierre Teilhard de Chardin. I am a christian, and I want to remain a christian and I want my children to have that privilege also. Therefore my faith is in Jesus Christ as the one with whom God in accordance with the scriptures and the natural order shared a human existence, and in whom God in accordance with the scriptures and the natural order expressed himself in terms of a human personality. With such a faith I can live and work in the same world as physicists and psychiatrists, with muslims and with buddhists, and be aware of my brotherhood in depth with all men of good will everywhere.

This, then, is where I stand and what I understand. I recognise the unity of the universe, and I am aware of the life-force inherent in it; that is, I believe in God. Because of my own nature, and my sense of the inalienable rights which the personal level of being bestows upon me, I believe God himself to be not less than personal. I further believe that I am encouraged to grow in personality because he seeks to know me and to have me know him. In the universe at large he is working out purposes too vast for human kind as yet to grasp; when or if we are able to visit other worlds we may learn more. But in this world, at least, God is working his purpose out in evolution and human history. This understanding first came to the Hebrews, and he entered into their history, and thus into that of all mankind, in the person of Jesus of Nazareth. The life and death of Jesus explicates for me the nature and the possibility of the Kingdom. It is this Kingdom that I must strive to enter, and the 'Open Secret' of the Gospel is that I may hope to do so by the lively assistance of the Holy Spirit, who is also Jesus living and active in his Church. In that Church I am already at the doors of the Kingdom, which is to be, in one of its aspects at least, the human community living as God would have us live.

Here then I stand, like the ancient prophet on his watch-tower, but my vantage point is a shrinking planet in an expanding universe; here I stand, like a surf-rider, precariously poised in the sweeping wave of the on-rush of human knowledge; here I stand, knocking on the door of the Kingdom of God, knowing that it will be opened. It is all very exciting.

INDEX OF NAMES